Praise for
Books from The Planning Shop

"User-friendly and exhaustive…highly recommended. Abrams' book works because she tirelessly researched the subject. Most how-to books on entrepreneurship aren't worth a dime; among the thousands of small business titles, Abrams' [is an] exception."

— *Forbes*

"There are plenty of decent business-plan guides out there, but Abrams' was a cut above the others I saw. *The Successful Business Plan* won points with me because it was thorough and well organized, with handy worksheets and good quotes. Also, Abrams does a better job than most at explaining the business plan as a planning tool rather than a formulaic exercise. Well done."

— *Inc.*

"Abrams' book offers a complete approach to creating your plan. Surrounding her explanatory material with commentary from top CEOs, venture capitalists, and business owners, Abrams helps you see your idea through the eyes of potential investors. Her book and your idea deserve each other."

—*Home Office Computing*

"This book stands head and shoulders above all other business plan books, and is the perfect choice for the beginner and the experienced business professional. Rhonda Abrams turns writing a professional, effective business plan into a journey of discovery about your business."

—*BizCountry*

"If you'd like something that goes beyond the mere construction of your plan and is more fun to use, try *The Successful Business Plan: Secrets and Strategies*, by Rhonda Abrams…this book can take the pain out of the process."

— *"Small Business School,"*
PBS television show

"I would not use any other book for my course on Business Development. *The Successful Business Plan* is the best I've ever seen, read, or used in a classroom environment."

— *Prof. David Gotaskie,*
Community College of Allegheny County,
Pittsburgh, PA

Business Plan In A Day

Get it done right, get it done fast™

Rhonda Abrams
with Julie Vallone

thePlanningshop

PALO ALTO, CALIFORNIA

Business Plan In A Day: Get it done right, get it done fast™

©2005 by Rhonda Abrams. Published by The Planning Shop™

ISBN 13: 978-0974-08012-3
ISBN: 0-9740801-2-8

Cover and interior design: Arthur Wait, Diana Van Winkle
Project Editor: Mireille Majoor

Services for our readers

Colleges, business schools, corporate purchasing:

The Planning Shop offers special discounts and supplemental materials for universities, business schools, and corporate training. Contact:

info@PlanningShop.com

or call 650-289-9120

Free business tips and information

To receive Rhonda's free email newsletter on starting and growing a successful business, sign up at:

www.PlanningShop.com

The Planning Shop™
555 Bryant Street, #180
Palo Alto CA 94301 USA
650-289-9120

Fax: 650-289-9125
Email: info@PlanningShop.com
www.PlanningShop.com

The Planning Shop™ is a division of Rhonda, Inc., a California corporation.

"This publication is designed to provide accurate and authoritative information in regard to the subject matter covered. It is sold with the understanding that the publisher and author are not engaged in rendering legal, accounting, or other professional services. If legal advice or other expert assistance is required, seek the services of a competent professional."
—from a Declaration of Principles, jointly adopted by a committee of the American Bar Association and a committee of publishers

Printed in Canada

10 9 8 7 6 5 4 3 2

About
Rhonda Abrams

A syndicated columnist, best-selling author, and popular public speaker, Rhonda Abrams has spent more than fifteen years advising, mentoring, and consulting with entrepreneurs and small business owners. Her knowledge of the small business market and her passion for entrepreneurship have made her one of the nation's most recognized advocates for small business.

Rhonda's weekly newspaper column, "Successful Business Strategies," is the nation's most widely read column about entrepreneurship, reaching more than twenty million readers through USATODAY.com, Inc.com, *Costco Connection* magazine, and 130 newspapers.

Rhonda's first book, *The Successful Business Plan: Secrets & Strategies*, was acclaimed by *Forbes* magazine as one of the two best books for small business and by *Inc.* magazine as one of the six best books for start-ups. Now in its fourth edition, it is used as the primary text for business plan classes by more than one hundred business schools.

Rhonda's subsequent books include:

- *Six-Week Start-Up,* helping entrepreneurs launch a business quickly and successfully by taking them week-by-week through the details of starting a business

- *Wear Clean Underwear*, illuminating how great values make great companies

- *What Business Should I Start?* guiding would-be entrepreneurs through a thoughtful process to identify the right business for them

Books by Rhonda Abrams have been translated into Chinese, Japanese, Korean, Dutch, Portuguese, and Russian.

An experienced entrepreneur, Rhonda has started three successful companies, including a small business planning consulting firm. Her experience gives her a strong real-life understanding of the challenges facing entrepreneurs. Currently, she is the founder and CEO of The Planning Shop, a company focused on providing entrepreneurs with high-quality information and tools for developing successful businesses.

Rhonda was educated at Harvard University and UCLA. She lives in Palo Alto, California.

The *In A Day* Promise
Get it done right, get it done fast

You're busy. We can help.

The Planning Shop is dedicated to helping entrepreneurs create and grow successful businesses. As entrepreneurs ourselves, we understand the many demands placed on you. We don't assume that you're a dummy, just that you're short on time.

This *In A Day* book will enable you to complete a critical business task in a hurry —and in the right way. You'll get it done right and get it done fast.

Can you complete this project in just twenty-four hours? Yes. Perhaps the twenty-four hours won't be consecutive. You may start—pause for an hour, day, or week to take care of other business—then return to the task later. Or, you may have some research or other preparation to do before you can complete this project.

We'll guide you through the process, show you what you absolutely have to do, and give you tips and tricks to help you reach your goals. We've talked to the experts and done the research so you don't have to. We've also eliminated any unnecessary steps so you don't waste your valuable time. That's the *In A Day* promise.

When you have a business task you need to do *now*, The Planning Shop's *In A Day* books will help you get it done—in as little as a day.

Need a Business Plan Fast?
This Book Is For You!

You need a business plan—fast!

Maybe a potential investor has asked to see your plan by Tuesday. Perhaps you need a business plan to present at an upcoming staff meeting. Possibly you just want to get your business off the ground as quickly as possible.

Business Plan In A Day was created for busy people like you. This book delivers the critical, time-tested information and tools you need to develop a well-constructed and effective plan—quickly and efficiently.

Business Plan In A Day was designed to help you successfully achieve your goal. It's for people who need a business plan to:

- Seek financing from a bank or other lender
- Approach investors, such as angel investors or venture capitalists
- Create a new business
- Expand an existing business
- Report to management on department or team plans
- Set goals with, inform, and motivate team members or employees
- Enter a business plan competition or complete a college business plan project
- Plan the strategy and direction of a company

An effective business plan saves you time and money by focusing your business activities. It can give you control over your finances, marketing, and daily operations. A good plan can also help you raise the money you need to build your company. *Business Plan In A Day* gives you everything you need to get it done right—and get it done fast!

Not sure what business to start?

Find tips and suggestions in The Planning Shop's *What Business Should I Start?*, available at bookstores or for online purchase at: **www.PlanningShop.com**.

Want to learn more about business concepts and business plans?

For even more on business planning and business plans, see *The Successful Business Plan*, available at bookstores or for online purchase at: **www.PlanningShop.com**.

Overview:
What's a Business Plan?

Your business plan is a powerful document telling the story of your company. It presents your current position, your vision for the future, and your plans for realizing that vision.

A business plan answers the following questions:

- What is your business idea or what is your existing business?

- Who are your existing and/or potential customers and what motivates them to buy from you?

- How will you let your customers know about your business?

- Who are your competitors and how are you different from them?

- How will you carry out the basic functions of your business?

- Is your management team capable of guiding your business to success?

- What is the long-range future of your business?

- What is your company's financial picture? How much money will it cost to run your business and how much money will you make?

Anatomy of a Business Plan

The basic parts of a complete business plan are:

- **Executive Summary**: Highlights the most important aspects of your business, summarizing key points of your business plan.

- **Company Description:** Features the basic, factual details about your business.

- **Target Market Description:** Identifies the types of people or businesses most likely to be your customers, and explains their needs and wants.

- **Competitive Analysis**: Evaluates other companies offering a similar product or service or filling a similar market need.

- **Marketing and Sales Plan:** Outlines how you will reach your customers and secure orders or make sales.

- **Operations Plan**: Explains how you run your business and the operational factors that may give you an edge over your competition.

- **Management Team:** Describes the key people running your business.

- **Development Plan and Milestones:** Shows where your business will be in several years' time, how you will get there, and the milestones you plan to reach along the way.

- **Financials.** A set of financial statements showing the current financial status and future financial goals of your company.

Although the Executive Summary appears first in your plan, prepare it last. You'll find it much easier to put together when you can draw from the highlights of each previously completed section.

Business Plan In A Day guides you quickly and efficiently through the process of developing a business plan. It's a roadmap to your success.

Time-Saving Tools

You probably already have a number of documents that will enable you to complete your plan faster. These include:

Industry information, statistics, and data

- Surveys and other research about your target customers
- Information about your competition, including research from their Web sites
- Marketing brochures and other marketing materials
- Any past internal company planning papers
- Past tax returns (for existing companies)
- Organizational charts
- Charts depicting operational procedures
- Product data sheets

At the beginning of each step in this book, you'll find checklists showing the kinds of documents and other materials likely to provide helpful information for each section.

Using the Book

Throughout this book you'll see samples from the business plan of the fictional company ComputerEase. Next to them you'll find worksheets where you can jot down and organize the information about your own company. By the time you finish each worksheet, you'll have all the information necessary for your own business plan.

The ComputerEase sample plan sections (based on a fictional company) illustrate how particular sections of a completed business plan might look. The sample plans are in an abbreviated form due to space limitations; your own plan may be longer.

MARKET TRENDS

The economic base of the Greater Vespucci area has been expanding. According to the Census Bureau, in the last four years the number of paid employees in the area has increased by over 50,000. A survey by the local newspaper, the *Vespucci Explorer*, showed that 43% of larger companies intended to add employees in the next twenty-four months.

Promising trends

Use the worksheets to write down the information about your own company you'll need to complete your plan. If there's not enough space on the worksheets, use a separate piece of paper to record your thoughts and data.

What is the rate of growth of your target market?

What changes are occurring in the makeup of the market? (Include changes in technology, the economy, social values and concerns.)

Electronic versions of the financial worksheets found in Step 9 are available for download purchase at: **www.PlanningShop.com**.

How to
Use This Book

Business *Plan In A Day* outlines the key elements of a business plan in a step-by-step guide, showing you what to include—and what to leave out—in every section of your plan. Within each step, you'll find the tools to help you complete your own personal plan, including:

- Checklists outlining what you will accomplish in each step

- "Time-Saving Tools" showing what information, if you have it, will let you finish the task faster

- Worksheets that help you organize data about your own company for each section of your plan

- A sample business plan showing what the parts of your plan might look like

- QuickTips, Sidebars, and Keys to Success to help you make certain your plan is done right

At the end of the book, we show you how to put it all together. A presentation and layout section explains how you can design your plan to achieve the best results.

You'll also find interviews with four experts who read and judge business plans every day—a banker, a venture capitalist, and two angel investors. These real-life professionals give valuable insight into what makes a winning plan, and they share the common mistakes that can lead to rejection.

Finally, a "Resources" section helps you locate a funding source for your venture by offering a list of groups and associations that provide business financing, as well as a variety of resources for entrepreneurs.

From the step-by-step plan-building guidelines to the valuable "Keys to Success," *Business Plan In A Day* is your one-stop resource for creating a successful business plan. Our goal: to help get your plan done, get it done right, and get it done fast.

Business Plan In A Day
Contents

1

STEP 1: **Executive Summary**

Accomplishments

In this step you'll:

☐ 1. Prepare your Executive Summary

Time-Saving Tools

You'll complete this section more quickly if you have any of the following handy:

☐ Information about your potential business plan readers

☐ Completed worksheets for Steps 2-9

Step 1:
Executive Summary

Your Executive Summary is the single most important part of your business plan—particularly if you are seeking outside funding. Busy investors and lenders start reading here and use the Executive Summary to get an understanding of your business quickly.

In fact, some investors ask entrepreneurs to first send only their Executive Summary and financial statements (Step 9). If they like what they see, they'll request the full plan. So if you can hook your readers here, they'll ask for more. Your goal is to both summarize the major components of your business and to make your readers want to learn more.

This doesn't mean you can misrepresent your business. As in all parts of your business plan, the information and data you present in your Executive Summary must be truthful. But you can, and should, focus on those aspects of your business that show it in the very best light.

Your Executive Summary provides a *brief* snapshot of your business. Highlight the most important facts and concepts from your full business plan as concisely as possible. When completed, your Executive Summary will answer these questions for your readers:

- Does your basic concept make sense?
- Has your business been thoroughly planned?
- Is the management team capable?
- Is there a clear-cut market need for your product/service?
- What advantages do you have over your competition?
- Are your financial projections realistic?
- Is the business likely to succeed?
- Will investors be able to make money? Will lenders be able to get their money back?

Visualize your reader

As you create your Executive Summary, ask yourself, "Who's going to read my business plan?" You can improve your chances of getting a positive reaction if you keep your potential business plan reader in mind as you write.

Remember, your reader is only going to spend a few minutes on your Executive Summary. They're going to hone in on the issues that concern them most. If you understand their priorities, you'll be better able to craft it to push just the right buttons.

Do some homework to discover the interests and concerns of your likely business plan reader. Then put those issues near the top of your Executive Summary. A venture capitalist might want to see that you have ground-breaking new technology, and an angel investor might want to see that you've identified an easily reached target market, while a banker wants to know that the company owners are investing their own money in the business. Give more emphasis to those aspects that concern your reader most.

Of course, you might not be able to identify the particular person who's going to read your plan. In that case, you can focus on the *type* of person and their concerns. For instance, a banker is likely to look for aspects of your business plan that minimize risk, since they want to make sure their loan will be secure. An investor, on the other hand, looks for aspects that increase the chance that your company will grow large, since they will get a piece of the action. Refer to the interviews with investors and lenders in *The Experts Talk* on pages 155-169 to get a better idea of how each type of reader reviews business plans.

QUICK**TIP**

What Sets You Apart?

Think about the number of business plans your readers must plow through each day, especially if they're investors or bank lenders. (An average venture capitalist, for instance, usually sees about 1,000 plans a year.) What distinguishes yours from the rest of the stack? Highlight the qualities that set you apart from all the other businesses early on in your Executive Summary. Put your winning concept up front and make sure your readers get it.

1. Prepare your summary

Your Executive Summary is the single most important part of your business plan. Readers will review it before they read any other section. Many readers will breeze through the Executive Summary, so you need to explain your business concept clearly, concisely, and in a way that makes them want to know more. Your Executive Summary is the first impression many readers will get of your company. Make sure it's a good one.

On pages 8-10, you'll find a worksheet to help you prepare your Executive Summary. Each question on the worksheet refers to corresponding worksheets throughout this book. You'll find it much easier—and quicker—to complete the Executive Summary worksheet if you've already worked through the rest of the steps in this book (Steps 2-9). Just refer to your completed worksheets to assemble the key ingredients for an informative, compelling Executive Summary.

Before you get to the worksheets you'll see a sample Executive Summary for the fictional company ComputerEase. Review this model for more ideas about the content and structure of an Executive Summary.

⚙ KEY TO SUCCESS

Pay Attention to Presentation!

A few ways to make your Executive Summary look appealing to readers:

- **Divide the Summary into paragraphs that mirror the sections of your business plan.**

- **Keep each topic brief.**

- **Use bullets to highlight your most compelling information.**

- **Include a small chart or graph if it makes an important point clear.**

- **Use white space and informative subheads to break up text blocks and make the pages seem less intimidating.**

For additional suggestions, see *Presentation Pointers* on page 141.

EXECUTIVE SUMMARY

Immediately highlights a positive factor

THE COMPANY

ComputerEase, Incorporated, an Indiana-based company, provides computer software training services to corporations in the greater Vespucci, Indiana, area. The technology-related business services industry is one of the fastest growing in America, and ComputerEase intends to capitalize on that growth. The company's stock is currently held by President and CEO Scott E. Connors and Susan Alexander, Vice President, Marketing.

Provides basic company details in a straightforward style

PRODUCTS AND SERVICES

The company provides software training programs targeted to the corporate market. Classes are conducted either at the customer's place of business or at ComputerEase's Corporate Training Center. Additionally, weekend classes are offered to the general public. Training is offered for all leading software programs. ComputerEase will also devise custom programs at corporate customers' request.

Briefly describes the company's offerings

TARGET MARKET

ComputerEase operates in the greater Vespucci, Indiana, area, targeting large- and medium-sized businesses with high computer use. Vespucci is the sixteenth-largest city in the United States, with a diverse and healthy economy. U.S. Census Bureau data show that more than 10,000 companies and institutions with more than fifty employees (ComputerEase's primary target market) are located in the area.

Shows large market potential

THE COMPETITION

No market leaders have yet emerged in the corporate software training field in the Vespucci region. Competition is diverse and uneven, creating substantial market opportunities. ComputerEase maintains the following advantages over existing competition: company-owned, up-to-date computer training center; local sales staff with strong ties to target customers; certification and strategic partnerships with leading software publishers; ongoing post-training customer support.

Describes competitive edge

MARKETING AND SALES STRATEGY

ComputerEase differentiates itself in its marketing by emphasizing the needs of the corporation, not merely the students in the training classes. The company employs a highly regarded sales professional with extensive ties to the target market. ComputerEase secures sales predominantly through face-to-face solicitation, unlike national competitors who rely on mail or phone solicitations.

OPERATIONS

ComputerEase owns its own Corporate Training Center with twelve personal computer stations fully equipped with all the latest versions of the most-used business software programs. The company offers corporate training sessions at the Center, as well as at the customer's place of business. It plans to open a second Training Center with funds currently being sought. ComputerEase utilizes the excess capacity of the Training Center by offering Saturday classes to consumers. All equipment is leased, resulting in lower capital expenses and ensuring the latest in equipment at all times.

MANAGEMENT

President and Founder Scott E. Connors brings significant technology-related management experience to this position. Immediately before starting ComputerEase, Connors served as regional vice president for Wait's Computer Emporium, a large computer hardware and electronics retail chain. Earlier, he was a sales representative for IBM. Vice President Susan Alexander brings direct experience in marketing to, and contacts with, the target market from her prior position as assistant marketing director for AlwaysHere Health Care Plan and sales experience as sales representative for SpeakUp Dictation Equipment.

Highlights management's relevant experience

DEVELOPMENT

In the future, the company may become a franchise operation, or expand its own company owned and operated training centers throughout the Midwest region. The company's goal is to become the dominant regional corporate software training provider.

FINANCIALS

The financial strategy of ComputerEase emphasizes reinvestment of income for growth during the first few years of operation, with the company reaching profitability by year three. Annual revenue projections for the current year are $233,000; for year two, $493,875; and for year three, $818,615.

FUNDS SOUGHT AND USES

The company is currently seeking $80,000 in investment financing. These funds will be used for expansion activities, including opening an additional Training Center, hiring new staff, and increasing marketing activities. Long-term plans call for the company to either develop a franchise operation or expand to become a regional chain, adding at least one training location annually. The company would then also be an excellent candidate for acquisition by a national training company.

Provides specific numbers and uses of funds. Hints at exit opportunity

What is your business all about? What are its most compelling qualities? Answer the questions on this worksheet, summarizing conclusions you've reached in the worksheets in Steps 2-9 of this book. Organize the information in a way that most appeals to your target reader. Combine related topics if that improves the flow.

THE COMPANY

What are the basic details of your business? (See worksheets on pages 15 and 17.)

_____

_____

_____

_____

_____

_____

PRODUCTS AND SERVICES

What products/services do you offer or plan to offer? (See worksheet on page 21.)

_____

_____

_____

_____

_____

TARGET MARKET

Who are your customers? (Include a summary of any market research results.)
(See worksheet on page 42.)

_____

_____

_____

_____

_____

_____

_____

THE COMPETITION

Who are your competitors? How is the market currently divided? What gives your company its competitive edge? (See worksheet on page 58.)

MARKETING AND SALES STRATEGY

How will you market and sell your product? (See worksheet on page 70.)

OPERATIONS

What are your most important operational features? (See worksheet on page 82.)

MANAGEMENT

Who are your founders? Who are the key members of your management team and what are their qualifications? (See worksheet on page 96.)

DEVELOPMENT

What is the company's current stage of development? What are your long-term goals? What are some of the milestones you've met or plan to meet? What is your potential exit strategy? (See worksheet on page 110.)

FINANCIALS

What are the expected financial highlights/performance of your company? What are your company's expected gross sales and net profits? (Use gross sales and net profit figures from the worksheets on pages 122-123.)

FUNDS SOUGHT AND USES

How much money are you seeking, from what sources, and how will the money be used? (See worksheets on pages 25 and 137.)

Accomplishments

In this step you'll:

- ☐ 1. List your company's name(s) and·location(s)
- ☐ 2. Provide information about your company's ownership and legal structure
- ☐ 3. Describe your company's history, development stage, and milestones
- ☐ 4. Describe your product(s) and service(s)
- ☐ 5. Give an overview of your industry
- ☐ 6. Explain how your company has been funded to date and how much money you are seeking

Time-Saving Tools

You'll complete this section more quickly if you have any of the following handy:

- ☐ Business license(s), incorporation papers, or other key business documents
- ☐ Legal and financial agreements
- ☐ Product or service descriptions
- ☐ Dates of key developments in your company's history
- ☐ Industry research data

Step 2:
Company Description

The Company Description provides the basic details about your business. While your Executive Summary creates a compelling case for why your business will succeed, the Company Description fills in the necessary specifics.

While much of this information seems—and is—mundane, providing these facts is the foundation of the picture you paint of your company. Completing this section should not be particularly time consuming or cumbersome; the goal is to quickly provide background information about your company's structure, ownership, and developments to date.

This section also provides a glimpse of what's going on in your industry. Offering an overview of your industry is particularly important if it is going through significant changes or facing economic difficulties. You'll need to show you understand the challenges your business, as part of that industry, faces. Of course, if your industry is healthy and growing, you'll want to point out those positive trends.

1. Give your company name(s) and location(s)

In the introductory section of your company description, include the basic details you'd put on any business application or form.

To begin, provide all the names associated with your company. In many cases, the name of your company or corporation is not the same as the name(s) you use when doing business with the public. You may actually have a number of different "names" associated with your business, including:

- Your own name

- If incorporated, the corporation name

- A DBA—or "doing business as"—also known as a "fictitious business name"

- Brand name(s)

- The name of your Web site

- Subsidiary companies

For instance, a restaurant called "Carla's Trattoria" might be legally owned by a corporation named C & J Food Enterprises. "Carla's Trattoria" is the DBA of the company, and both names should be listed in the business plan. If the restaurant's owners also bottle and sell spaghetti sauce, the name of the brand of their bottled foods ("Carla's Special Sauces") should also be listed.

List the location of your company's main place of business, any branch locations, and any other locations, such as warehouses. If you operate more than two or three branches, you can list the total number of locations here, but include a complete list of addresses in your business plan's appendix.

COMPANY NAME AND LOCATION

ComputerEase, Inc., is an Indiana-based company providing computer software training services to business customers in the greater Vespucci, Indiana, area, operating under the name "ComputerEase."

Corporate headquarters and the company's software training classrooms are located at 987 South Main Street, Vespucci, Indiana. ComputerEase also offers software training classes at its corporate clients' offices.

Name(s) of business

Company address and location where they conduct business

What are the names associated with your company? (List all company names, including the legal name of the corporation, "DBA," brand or product names, names of subsidiaries, and domain names.)

Where is the company's main place of business? (Give the specific address, if known, or the general area or city if a location is yet to be selected.)

Do you have more than one location? (If so, list the addresses of each. If the company has many locations, list the total number and addresses or areas where they're located.)

2. Provide information about your company's ownership and legal status

Who owns your company? If yours is a one-person business, the answer may be simple: you do. But if you have gone into business with others, you need to spell out the ownership division and indicate the names of all major shareholders.

It's also important to specify the legal form of your business, especially if you're seeking financing. Your funders want to know what type of entity they're doing business with. Many businesses often start out as one form of business (such as sole proprietor) and decide to incorporate later.

Other legal considerations to note here include:

- Licensing and distribution agreements

- Trademarks, copyrights, patents

- Other legal protections you have secured to protect your proprietary business assets

- Other legal issues having a major impact on your business

What's Your Legal Status?

Sole Proprietorship: The company is not incorporated and is owned and managed by one person.

Partnership: A relationship in which two or more people own a company, sharing profits, losses, and, usually, management. You can legally be deemed to be in a partnership even if you have not drawn up legal partnership documents.

C Corporation: A corporate form allowing a greater number and diversity of shareholders than other corporate forms. Corporate income is taxed before profits or losses are distributed to shareholders.

Subchapter S Corporation: A small corporation limited in the number and type of shareholders. It provides the liability protection of a C Corporation, but profits and losses are "passed through" to the owners' personal tax returns.

Limited Liability Company (LLC) or Limited Liability Partnership (LLP): A legal form of business offering benefits similar to those of a Subchapter S Corporation but often with less cost and paperwork.

OWNERSHIP AND LEGAL STATUS

ComputerEase was incorporated in the state of Indiana one year ago. Ten thousand shares in the company have been issued: 6,000 are owned by President and CEO Scott E. Connors; 1,000 are owned by Vice President of Marketing, Susan Alexander; and 3,000 shares have been retained by the company for future distribution.

The company was granted the trademark "ComputerEase" by the U.S. Patent and Trademark Office.

Status as a corporate entity

Indicates percent of ownership by each owner

Another important legal consideration

What is the legal form of your business? (Sole proprietorship? Partnership? C Corporation? Subchapter S Corporation? LLC?) **If it is incorporated, in which state or province?**

_____

_____

_____

Who owns your company? If the company has more than one owner, what percentage of the company does each own? If the company is incorporated, who owns the stock and in what amounts?

_____

_____

_____

What trademarks, copyrights, or patents does the company hold?

_____

_____

_____

What other important legal issues affect the company? (Distribution or licensing agreements? Major lawsuits? Regulatory concerns?)

_____

_____

_____

QUICK**TIP**

**Examples of
Key Milestones**

- Incorporation

- Prototype completed

- First product shipped

- Major customers secured

- Key strategic partnerships
  secured

- Significant sales level
  reached

3. Describe your company's history, development stage, and milestones

Your company's history and milestones may make up the bulk of the Company Description portion of your business plan. In this section, you present the history and progress of your company.

First, indicate which phase of development your business is in. The basic stages are:

- **Seed company**. The business concept is developed, but the product or service is not yet finalized. Not yet making sales.

- **Start-up**. In the early stages of operation. Securing first customers.

- **Expanding**. Established company adding new products, services, or branches. Rapidly increasing sales growth.

- **Stable**. Established company with modest ongoing sales growth.

- **Retrenchment**. Consolidating or repositioning product lines. Little or no sales growth.

Next, indicate the progress you've already made. Even if yours is a new business, you've almost certainly reached key milestones, such as developing a product prototype, securing seed financing, or finding office space. Be sure to include development details that indicate you're off to a good start.

If your company is up and running, you already have some major accomplishments under your belt, such as reaching significant sales levels, securing major customers, or shipping products. Highlight these in this portion of your Company Description.

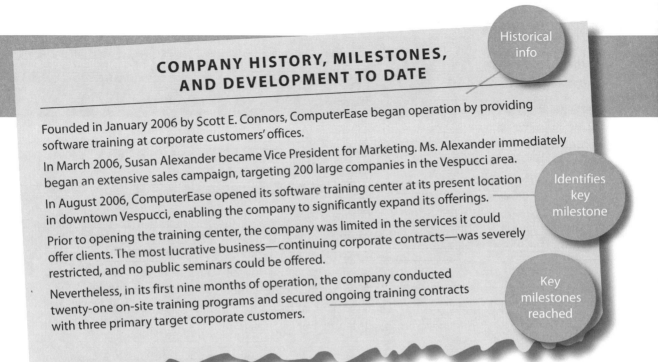

COMPANY HISTORY, MILESTONES, AND DEVELOPMENT TO DATE

Historical info

Founded in January 2006 by Scott E. Connors, ComputerEase began operation by providing software training at corporate customers' offices.

In March 2006, Susan Alexander became Vice President for Marketing. Ms. Alexander immediately began an extensive sales campaign, targeting 200 large companies in the Vespucci area.

In August 2006, ComputerEase opened its software training center at its present location in downtown Vespucci, enabling the company to significantly expand its offerings.

Identifies key milestone

Prior to opening the training center, the company was limited in the services it could offer clients. The most lucrative business—continuing corporate contracts—was severely restricted, and no public seminars could be offered.

Nevertheless, in its first nine months of operation, the company conducted twenty-one on-site training programs and secured ongoing training contracts with three primary target corporate customers.

Key milestones reached

When was your company founded?

_____

_____

_____

How would you describe your current phase of development? (Seed? Start-up? Expanding? Stable? Retrenchment?)

_____

_____

_____

What are some of the highlights of your company's history? What milestones have you reached so far?

_____

_____

_____

_____

QUICK**TIP**

Avoid Disclosing Sensitive Information

Be careful about putting highly proprietary or technical details in your plan, even if your reader has signed a non-disclosure agreement. You can present these details at a later stage of discussion.

4. Identify your product(s) or service(s)

Identify the specific types of products or services you sell. If you have a large product line or offer many services, you don't need to list each one separately. Instead, list the general categories.

For example, if you're opening a new gardening center, you don't need to list all the specific plants and products you'll sell, just the general nature of your merchandise: "a full line of plants for the home gardener, garden tools, planters and containers, plant food and chemicals, and a small selection of gardening books."

When describing a product or service, provide just enough detail to give a clear picture of what it is or does. Too much detail makes this section cumbersome for your readers.

However, if you're seeking financing for a new type of product or service, particularly one that is not immediately understandable to your readers, provide more information. A brief explanation of what you'll be making or doing is appropriate here. Reserve detailed descriptions of production processes for the Appendix of your business plan.

If you are changing the nature of your products or services, or plan to make changes in the future, describe the changes you anticipate. Explain why you plan to make the change— perhaps a new production method will result in cost savings —and how you expect your product/service line to differ over time.

SERVICES

ComputerEase offers training classes for users of all leading business software programs. The company also devises custom training programs for corporate clients. ComputerEase's classes are targeted primarily to the corporate market. Training classes are taught either on-site at the customers' offices or at ComputerEase's Training Center in downtown Vespucci. To take full advantage of the company's resources, training classes for the general public are taught on Saturday at the company's Training Center.

Range and nature of services provided

List your product(s) and/or service(s) and describe its function(s).

Product/Service	What It Does

What plans, if any, do you have to change your products or services in the future?

QUICK**TIP**

Sniffing Out Industry Info

Researching industry trends enables you to provide facts supporting your claims for your company's potential success. Let's say you're opening a doggie day spa. This idea might raise investor eyebrows. You'll help overcome their skepticism by providing data showing the dramatic increase in spending on pets in recent years. Even more convincing are sales figures for pet clothing boutiques, doggie day care centers, and specialty pet-food stores.

5. Describe your industry

No business is an island. Every business, including yours, operates as part of a larger overall industry. Forces affecting your industry as a whole will inevitably affect your business, as well.

Every industry changes. Some changes come about because the customers for the products or services change. For instance, aging baby boomers provide new opportunities for industries serving retirees or the elderly. Other industry changes occur because of new technology, outsourcing or offshoring, or corporate mergers.

Make sure you address the major changes occurring in your industry. Indicate how you're prepared to take advantage of the opportunities presented and respond appropriately to any challenges you face.

Pay particular attention to your industry's recent economic health and rate of growth. When looking for financing, potential funding sources ask tougher questions if you're in a troubled or shrinking industry than if you're in a healthy, expanding one.

INDUSTRY DEVELOPMENTS AND TRENDS

ComputerEase is well positioned to take advantage of the significant opportunities resented by the rapidly expanding industry of computer-related business services. From 2001-2005, the industry grew in excess of 125%, compared to an overall GDP increase of approximately 29.5% during that period.

Computer software training is a relatively new industry, an outgrowth of the phenomenal expansion of computer use. The industry is still in a state of flux, with no market leaders, creating the opportunity for newer, smaller companies to succeed.

The key to success in the industry is to develop regionally known companies, as is currently the case with other business services such as accounting or employment services. These regionally-dominant training companies are able to earn revenues and build market share sufficient to sustain the high overhead due to the cost of equipment, skilled trainers, and materials.

The current lack of industry leaders represents an opportunity for ComputerEase to develop a strong presence and client base in the Greater Vespucci area.

Healthy industry growth

Strategic opportunity

In what industry (or industries) does your company operate? What types of businesses belong to this industry?

Is your industry growing? What's the rate of growth?

What trends in the industry provide you with opportunities?

What challenges, if any, is your industry facing?

How do you plan to capitalize on these opportunities and/or overcome these challenges?

6. Explain your company's funding

The purpose of this section is to provide a brief explanation of your financing to date and, if you're seeking financing, to describe how much money you need and for what purposes. It's not meant to provide a total financial picture of your company. That will be seen later in your financial statements.

Don't go into specific details, such as your accounts receivable or payable, here. However, indicate any major sources of future funds already committed to you. For instance, if you have secured a three-year contract with a large customer that will generate significant annual income, this is a good place to highlight that fact.

If you're using your business plan to seek financing, indicate how much money you're looking for and how you plan to use the money you receive. You'll expand on this in your "Sources and Use of Funds" worksheet on page 137.

FUNDING TO DATE AND FUNDS SOUGHT

Funding of the company to date has come from the personal savings of Mr. Connors. This has amounted to a $30,000 investment and $20,000 in loans. In addition, the company has received a $15,000 loan from Mr. Connors' family members. All other funding has come from the income generated by sales.

The company is now seeking $80,000 from outside investors. These funds will be used to open an additional Training Center, hire trainers, add staff, and expand marketing activities.

Indicates personal financial commitment of owner

Planned use of additional financing

How has the company been funded to date? How much have the company owners invested?

Has the company received funding from any other sources? If so, how much and on what terms?

What other major sources of funds has the company had?

How much money is the company seeking now and for what purposes?

Pulling It All Together: Company Description

A concise Company Description serves as a clear and convenient summary of the basic details of your company. Your Company Description provides readers with the facts they need to know about your company before delving deeper into your plan.

Draw from the information you provided in the worksheets in this step to complete this final worksheet.

What is the name and location of your company? (See worksheet on page 15.)

_____

Who owns the company and what is its legal status? (See worksheet on page 17.)

_____

What is your company's current phase of development, and what milestones have you reached to date? (See worksheet on page 19.)

_____

_____

What products and/or services do you offer? (See worksheet on page 21.)

_____

_____

What is the current health of your industry what are the key trends? (See worksheet on page 23.)

_____

_____

How has your company been funded to date? If you're looking for financing, how much money are you seeking and for what purposes? (See worksheet on page 25.)

_____

_____

3

Accomplishments

In this step you'll:

- ☐ 1. Specify the geographic location of your target market
- ☐ 2. Describe the demographic characteristics of your customers
- ☐ 3. Explain customer motivations and needs
- ☐ 4. Determine the size of your market
- ☐ 5. Evaluate market trends

Time-Saving Tools

You'll complete this section more quickly if you have any of the following handy:

- ☐ Maps of your target market area
- ☐ Customer surveys
- ☐ Market research reports
- ☐ Industry research indicating market trends
- ☐ Books, magazines, and other media geared toward your target market
- ☐ Census data showing customer demographics

Step 3:
Target Market

Your success rides on your ability to meet the needs and desires of your customers. In Step 3, identify these customers—not the *specific* people or businesses, but the *types* of customers you expect to serve. This is your target market.

Your goal is to assure your readers that:

- These customers do exist

- You know exactly who they are and what they want

- There are enough of them to support your business

- They're ready for what you have to offer and will actually buy

Paint a clear and detailed portrait of your customers—who they are, where they're located, how they think, why they buy, and what they want. This makes it easier to show how you plan to respond to their needs.

Strong target market definitions are based on observable characteristics, backed by data and research. This section outlines the kinds of information to include in a convincing target market description. See tips on collecting market research data on pages 32-33. If you have already done some market research, you'll complete this section more quickly.

🔑 KEY TO SUCCESS

Creating a Credible Market Definition

A strong target market definition is:

Definable. It identifies the specific characteristics potential customers have in common.

Meaningful. These characteristics directly relate to purchasing decisions.

Sizable. The number of those potential customers is large enough to sustain your business.

Reachable. You can affordably and effectively market to them.

QUICK**TIP**

Target Market: Planet Earth?

If you're writing a plan for an Internet business, avoid defining the entire planet as your geographic market. Issues like fulfillment, language barriers, and differences in market demand are likely to eliminate some areas from your definition. For instance, if you're selling parkas online, you probably won't get too many orders from Tahiti.

1. Specify the geographic location of your target market

Provide details about the geographic location you're planning to serve. On the worksheet opposite, show where your customers live or where their businesses operate. Explain how other characteristics about the location affect your customers and your business.

If relevant to your business, include such information as:

- Neighborhood, city, state, province, region, country, or international region

- Density of the area (urban, suburban, or rural)

- Climate (hot weather, cold weather, sunny, rainy, snowy)

- Traffic patterns (busy intersection, pedestrian area)

At this point, you are simply describing your target market geographic area, but your ultimate goal is to show the impact of its location on your business, if any.

TARGET MARKET LOCATION

ComputerEase operates in the greater Vespucci, Indiana, area. The geographic area includes the incorporated cities of:

- Vespucci
- Abergel Peak
- Newman City

And the suburban communities (with business centers) of:

- Karen's Springs
- Gaspar
- Lake Arthur

Geographic description

What geographic area will your business serve? (City? Country? Region?)

_____

_____

_____

_____

What type of area is it? (Urban? Rural? Suburban?) **What's the population density?**

_____

_____

_____

What are some other details related to the area your business will serve?
(Climate conditions? Traffic patterns?)

_____

_____

_____

_____

_____

_____

Conducting Market Research

Get to know your customers or potential customers. Try these tips to gain insight into your customers' needs and desires and to gather data that supports your assumptions about your target market:

- Talk to people or businesses that are, or could be, your customers. Ask them about what they want and need as related to your business.

- Conduct surveys and focus groups. These can be as informal as going to a mall and asking questions of consumers. If your budget allows, hire a professional market research firm to conduct interviews.

- Examine the media that your customers read, listen to, or view. Most media outlets, including newspapers, magazines, and radio and television stations, keep detailed demographic profiles of their audience and know what interests them.

- Check Web sites your customers visit, especially those in which they share their views.

- Check your local library. Your librarian can point you to online databases and print resources that provide data on your customers.

- Pay a visit (or several visits) to your competitors' places of business. Check out their Web sites. Figure out what they do to attract and serve customers.

Get a Media Kit

Media outlets—magazines and newspapers, radio and TV stations—can be a good source of demographic and lifestyle info about their audiences. If you know your target customers are likely to read a particular magazine, call the publication and request an advertiser or media kit. Chances are, it will include demographic data you can use. Some publications put these kits right on their Web sites. (Follow the links for advertisers, often found in the "About Us" section.)

Getting the Dirt On Your Market

Ever wonder why there seem to be three or four fast-food joints at the same intersection? Or why, all of a sudden, not one but three office-supply stores open in the same community?

The answer is that they all rely on similar statistics to choose locations. They look for particular factors: population density, characteristics of nearby residents (such as age, gender, income), and number and type of existing local businesses.

Big corporations hire consulting firms to compile these statistics. You've got an even bigger consulting group doing it for you—free! The United States government, particularly the Census Bureau, compiles a great deal of data useful for businesses, as does the Canadian government.

A few key websites for finding market data:

www.census.gov: U.S. Census Bureau. The entry page for all U.S. census data. Use this resource to access information about people, businesses, geography, trade, and much more.

http://quickfacts.census.gov: Quick Facts. An easy-to-use Web site providing quick access to a wide variety of information about population characteristics at the state or county level.

www.statscan.ca: Statistics Canada. The entry page for data about Canada compiled by the Canadian government. Choose "Community Profiles" to get detailed information about the population in a specific city or metropolitan area, including numbers, education levels, income levels, housing, and more.

http://canadianeconomy.gc.ca/english/economy: Canadian Economy Online. An entry point to data on a wide variety of Canadian economic-related topics, including population statistics, labor market conditions, family income and expenditures, and data on businesses by industry/sector.

QUICK**TIP**

Who's Your Customer?

Often, the person who purchases your product or service is not the same one who uses it. If you're selling to businesses, a purchasing department or supervisor may be the decision maker. If you're selling to consumers, a parent or spouse may be the decision maker and not the actual end user. You need to understand the needs and motivations of both the buyer and the ultimate end user.

2. Describe the demographic characteristics of your target customers

Discuss the observable, factual characteristics of your target customers—traits such as age, income level, family size, gender, and ethnic group. If you are targeting businesses rather than consumers, these characteristics would include traits such as which industries they're in, the size of the companies, and their stage of development (new business, expanding, or shrinking). Look for *meaningful* characteristics that directly relate to your customers' decisions to purchase.

Say you're opening an elite hair salon in Manhattan. You identify your primary target customers as single, college-educated, professional women, aged 35-50, with annual income levels ranging from $80,000-$150,000. These demographic details indicate this group has more money to spend on high-priced salon services and the motivation to spend it.

Using the worksheet opposite, fill in details on your target market. The more specific your details, the more credible your market definition.

TARGET CUSTOMER CHARACTERISTICS

ComputerEase primarily targets large- and medium-sized businesses with high computer use. They have:

- More than fifty employees
- High employee turnover
- An expanding number of employees
- A high dependence on computers

They are in the following industries:

- Government
- Insurance
- Financial/Banking
- Accounting
- Colleges and Universities
- Engineering
- Hospitals and other medical facilities
- Airlines

Demographic and business-style characteristics

ComputerEase conducted a market research survey with a selection of targeted companies. It showed:

- 42% of these companies have a "training" amount allotted in their current year's budget.

- 18% specifically have "computer or software training" budgeted for the current year.

- 34% have purchased software training services in the last year.

- 66% indicated they would purchase more training than at present if better-quality, more-reliable training were available.

What are general, observable traits of your customers (especially those related to their likelihood of buying your product/service)?

Consumer (Age? Income range? Gender? Occupation? Marital status? Family size? Education level? Hobbies?)

_____

_____

_____

_____

_____

_____

_____

_____

Business (Industries? Years in business? Revenues? Number of employees? Specific business needs?)

_____

_____

_____

_____

_____

_____

_____

_____

QUICK**TIP**

Marketing to Customer Perceptions

Research often shows differences between who your customers are (demographics, lifestyle, business style) and who they think they are or want to be. Customers' choices are based not only on reality, but on their perceptions of reality. Demonstrate how your business appeals to your customers by confirming and/or helping them move closer to their images of themselves.

3. Explain customer motivations and purchasing patterns

In addition to their observable demographic characteristics, highlight the less tangible, but no less real, factors influencing your customers' purchasing decisions. These include specific purchasing preferences, motivations based on how your customers view themselves, and how and when they actually buy.

When describing customer motivations, consider these questions:

- What concerns your customers most when making purchases? (Is it price? Quality? Convenience?)

- How quickly do they make their buying choices?

- Where do they usually buy their products or services?

- With what kinds of companies do they prefer to do business? (Large? Small? Socially responsible? Locally based?)

- How do your customers view themselves? (Do they see themselves as leading-edge? Technically savvy? Smart shoppers?)

When describing customer purchasing patterns, consider:

- Who makes the decision to purchase, if other than the end user?

- How often do they buy?

- How do they pay? (Cash? Credit? Purchase order? 30-60-90 day terms?)

Assess the organizational factors involved, especially if you are selling to other businesses. For example, large companies typically have formalized procurement systems, leading to slow purchasing decisions. This will affect the length of your sales cycle.

CUSTOMER MOTIVATIONS
AND PURCHASING PATTERNS

In the corporations that ComputerEase targets, the decision to purchase computer software training is typically made by the human resources director or department. It often takes six to twelve months for a decision to be made. The critical issues influencing the decision are quality of the training, reliability, and responsiveness to specific corporate needs. Price is a consideration, but typically not the primary one.

Management personnel view themselves as responsible and professional. They prefer to deal with service companies that present a stable, professional image. They're often considerably influenced by the fact that similar companies already use the service or product.

Buying patterns

Customer motivations

Self-image issues

What factors most influence your customers' purchasing decisions?

Consumer (Price? Brand? Customer service? Features? Packaging? Return policy?)

Business (Price? Reputation/stability of service provider? Fast delivery?)

How do your customers view themselves?

Consumer (Trend-setter? Good house keeper?)

Business (Industry leader? Fiscally prudent?)

How do your customers actually purchase your products or services?
Who makes the purchasing decision? Where and how frequently do they purchase?

Consumer

Business

QUICK**TIP**

Numbers, Numbers, Numbers

Your business plan will be more convincing with solid numbers describing the size of your target market. When your numbers come from a reliable source, numerical data shows you've done your homework. For U.S. companies, you'll find a surprisingly large amount of geographic and demographic data at the U.S. Census Bureau's Web site: *www.census.gov*. For additional resources, see The Planning Shop's *Successful Business Research*. (Available at bookstores or for online purchase at: www.PlanningShop.com.)

4. Determine your market size

Is your market big enough to keep you in business? You want to make sure your pool of potential customers is large enough to sustain you. If you're looking for investors, you need to convince potential funders that your company can grow to a size that will make their investment profitable.

On the other hand, is your market so large you could never reach it affordably? If your market is too large, you probably have not defined its specific characteristics well enough to be able to design an effective and affordable marketing and sales process. Be realistic about the size of your market and your ability to serve it.

For some businesses, especially smaller ones, determining whether your market size is sufficient will be mostly a matter of intuition. But if yours is a bigger company, or if you're seeking investors, gather data to support your plan.

Be Specific

It's tempting to include just about everyone in the definition of your target market; after all, couldn't the whole world benefit from your product or service? Not only is this unrealistic, it makes it seem as if you haven't really zeroed in on who your real customers are—or could be. By detailing specific characteristics of your target market, you give readers a clearer view of your customers. Doing this will also save you time and money in future marketing efforts.

MARKET SIZE

Vespucci and its surrounding communities make up a large and economically healthy area. According to census figures, the city of Vespucci has a population of approximately 675,000, making it the sixteenth-largest city in the U.S. The Vespucci Metropolitan Statistical Area (MSA) has an overall population approaching 1,500,000.

The business climate has been consistently strong due to Vespucci's diverse economic base. The Vespucci MSA includes three county seats and is the home to numerous government offices.

The Vespucci Chamber of Commerce estimates that, of the more than 10,000 companies and institutions with more than fifty employees in the Greater Vespucci area, at least 2,500 are in the primary industries targeted by ComputerEase.

Also located in the Greater Vespucci area are:

- An international airport
- The regional processing centers for three national insurance companies
- The data processing center for the state's highway patrol
- A state university and six other colleges and universities
- A major medical center

(Market size data)

(Additional geographic information)

What is the approximate size of your target market? (Include population of geographic area, if relevant, and total number of potential target customers.)

What other factors influence the size of the potential pool of customers?

QUICK**TIP**

**Check with
Your Suppliers**

Looking for insight into trends affecting your customers? Talk to your suppliers. They know who's buying what now and how these buying patterns have changed over time.

5. Evaluate market trends

Change happens. You can't be a fortune-teller, but the most successful companies stay aware of trends that can affect their businesses. Such trends include: a growing (or shrinking) population, a hiring boom (or layoffs) in your area, a shift in the kinds of people or businesses populating the area, and new technologies. In this section, highlight the trends in your market, especially those which will have a positive impact on your business. Address trends that are occurring both in your geographic area and among the types of customers you serve.

Trade Associations

Trade associations are excellent sources of information about both the current customers in an industry and trends affecting that industry. Check with your industry's trade association for studies and forecasts they've published. You can find a list of trade associations at The Planning Shop's website: **www.PlanningShop.com/ tradeassociations**.

MARKET TRENDS

The economic base of the Greater Vespucci area has been expanding. According to the Census Bureau, in the last four years the number of paid employees in the area has increased by over 50,000. A survey by the local newspaper, the *Vespucci Explorer*, has shown that 43% of larger companies intend to add employees in the next twenty-four months.

Promising trends

What is the rate of growth of your target market?

_____

_____

_____

_____

_____

_____

_____

_____

_____

What changes are occurring in the makeup of the market? (Include changes in technology, the economy, and in social values and concerns.)

_____

_____

_____

_____

_____

_____

_____

_____

Pulling It All Together: Target Market

A key part of creating your plan, and running your business, is understanding your customers—who they are, what they want, how they make their purchases. This information helps you more successfully design your products or services, develop your marketing, and secure sales.

Now that you're well acquainted with your target customers and their needs, pull together the highlights of your target market definition. Complete the worksheet below, choosing the most important and relevant information you've compiled in Step 3. You can reorder the information to highlight the most compelling aspects of your target market.

Where is your target market located? (See worksheet on page 31.)

What are the characteristics of your target customers? (See worksheet on page 35.)

What motivates your customers to make purchases and what are their buying patterns? (See worksheet on page 37.)

What is the size of your market? (See worksheet on page 39.)

What are some key market trends? (See worksheet on page 41.)

Accomplishments

In this step you'll:

- ☐ 1. Identify the types of competition you face
- ☐ 2. List your specific competitors
- ☐ 3. Determine market share distribution
- ☐ 4. Analyze the strength of your competitors
- ☐ 5. Highlight your competitive edge
- ☐ 6. Evaluate the barriers to entry and potential competition

Time-Saving Tools

You'll complete this section more quickly if you have any of the following handy:

- ☐ A list of major competitors
- ☐ Research on your competitors
- ☐ Industry or trade journal articles

Step 4:
The Competition

No matter what type of business you own or are planning to start, other companies want your customers. The fact that competition exists means you have tapped into a viable market with customers who want to buy the goods or services you have to sell. That's why other businesses, like yours, want to profit from them.

Even if you are trying to sell a new type of product, such as a groundbreaking new technology, expect competition. There may be no comparable product on the market, but there's probably something else that fits the market need. Take the photocopier, for instance. It was the first product of its kind but still faced competition. People were already duplicating documents using carbon paper and mimeograph machines.

The words "we have no competition" in a business plan indicate to potential investors that a) an entrepreneur hasn't fully examined the realities of the business, and/or b) no market exists for the concept. If you're sure you have a market, you can be sure you have competition.

In the short term, understanding—and describing—your competition helps you present a stronger case to your business plan readers. In the long term, keeping an eye on your competition keeps you on your toes and helps you build and run a better business.

Just as important as *knowing* your competition is *learning* from it. Watch what your competitors are doing right and doing wrong. That will show you how to better serve your potential customers and uncover strategic opportunities in the market.

1. Identify types of competition

What kinds of businesses contend with you for your customers' attention and dollars? Refer to *categories* of businesses here, rather than specific establishments. (You'll do that later.) For example, a clothing boutique might identify all similar boutiques within a ten-mile radius, *plus* well-known Web sites. An accountant might point to all other local accountants in town *as well as* popular accounting software programs. List these categories of competition, along with the strengths and weaknesses of each, on the worksheet opposite.

Types of Competition

You face two types of competition: direct and indirect.

Direct Competition: Companies offering products or services much like yours that customers perceive as acceptable alternatives (for example, Honda vs. Toyota or Burger King vs. McDonald's).

Indirect Competition: Companies offering products or services different from yours that meet the same or similar need. Customers can substitute your competitors' offerings for yours (for example, TV advertising vs. radio advertising, train travel vs. air travel, or a children's museum vs. Chuck E. Cheese's).

When developing this section, always consider less obvious sources of competition that attract your customers' attention and dollars.

TYPES OF COMPETITION

Competing with ComputerEase to supply software training services to the target market (businesses making substantial use of computers and having more than fifty employees) are these categories of software training providers:

- Individual independent training consultants
- Local software training companies
- National training companies
- Software developers
- Community college classes
- Trainers from within the targeted companies themselves
- Online distance learning/training programs

> Describes the range of competitors

ComputerEase does not intend to compete with training provided by software developers. Such software is usually highly specialized and training is often included in the cost of the software itself. Community college classes are generally not competitive in the marketplace; classes are held in the evenings for at least ten weeks, conditions that do not meet business customers' needs.

> Narrows the competitive field

List the types of businesses, not the specific companies, that compete with you. What are their strengths? What are their weaknesses?

Competition Type	Strengths	Weaknesses

QUICK**TIP**

Shop Your Competition

To collect valuable data and insights for your plan, spend time patronizing your competition. What attracts customers to them? How were you treated? Were their products reasonably priced? Visit your competitors' Web sites. What features or attributes do they highlight? Get to know your competition through their customers' eyes.

2. Identify your specific competitors

Zero in on specific businesses that compete for your customers on a day-to-day basis (such as the boutique down the street or another neighborhood accountant). Evaluate them in the same way you did your categories of competitors, based on how customers view them and how they operate.

Also note other attributes that may affect their ability to compete, such as:

- Do they have a well-known brand?
- Have they historically been the market leaders?
- Have they been growing?
- Are their marketing efforts focused specifically on your geographic target area?
- Do they have any strategic partnerships with other companies that give them marketing or operational advantages?
- Do they have any exclusive sales or distribution relationships?

Honestly evaluate your competitors. Resist the temptation to dismiss their products or services as inferior to yours. After all, there's a reason they're still in business.

Evaluating Your Competitors

Many factors beyond product quality and price come into play when evaluating competitors. Here are the two main categories of competitive factors:

Customer Perception Factors. Things customers can see. What product/service/company attributes make your competitors attractive or unattractive to your customers? These include: price, quality, customer service, and social consciousness.

Internal Operational Factors. Things customers can't see. What operational aspects put your competitors in a stronger or weaker position? Operational aspects include: labor costs, marketing budget and expertise, location, access to suppliers, and strategic partnerships.

Consider both types of factors when completing the worksheets on pages 47 and 49.

SPECIFIC COMPETITORS

Eight local businesses and four individuals in the Vespucci area actively market their software training services. An unknown number of additional individual consultants provide such training on a less visible level.

Only one local company has developed a substantial presence with the target market: JMT Training. JMT has operated for more than six years and is the largest local software training company.

The individual independent consultants generally provide training for just one or two software programs. Only one consultant, Seth Rose, has a meaningful corporate client base for his well-regarded spreadsheet training programs.

Other Competition
Three major national software training companies periodically conduct classes in the Vespucci area. Lesser-known national companies also occasionally provide such services, generally targeting recent purchasers of particular software. Online training is relatively new, with little or no market acceptance.

In-house training taught by employees of the targeted companies varies widely in content, form, and quality. Very few companies have "trainers"; most training is provided on an ad hoc basis from supervisors and fellow workers. A conservative interpretation of ComputerEase survey results indicate that at least 20% of such training would be contracted out if satisfactory training could be obtained.

Available, but insignificant, training resources

Field narrowed to just two significant competitors

What specific businesses (local, national, worldwide, and online) do you consider to be your direct competition? List them here by name, along with their strengths, weaknesses, and other notable attributes.

Competitor	Strengths	Weaknesses	Other Attributes

QUICK**TIP**

No Market Leader? Lucky for You!

It's difficult to unseat companies that already control a significant share of a market. Want to introduce a new cola-flavored soft drink? It's not easy getting customers away from Coke or Pepsi. You'd have better luck launching an energy drink. Entering a field where market share is widely divided—without clear leaders—gives you a better chance of getting a piece of an emerging market.

3. Determine your competitors' market share

Some competitors are more important than others. In particular, companies commanding the largest share of customers' dollars—in other words, "market share"—present the fiercest competition. Even though these companies may not necessarily provide the best products or most attentive customer service, they're going to be hard to beat. If you're opening a neighborhood hardware store, you're going to have to watch what's going on at Home Depot and Lowe's.

In this section, determine which companies command the largest portion of your market. These competitors are significant because they:

- Tend to define the standard features of a product or service
- Significantly influence customer perceptions of the product or service
- Usually have and spend the resources required to maintain their market share
- Can undercut prices to maintain market share

On the worksheet opposite, list your major competitors along with the percentage of the market each one commands (in revenues and/or units sold). Indicate whether their market share is increasing or decreasing. If yours is an existing business, indicate your market share.

Where to Find Market-Share Data

Trade associations, corporate annual reports, business publications, and independent research firms provide helpful sources of general data to use for your market share section. Many university libraries have business databases and print resources available. The Planning Shop's *Successful Business Research* can direct you to specific sources of market-share data. (Available at bookstores or for online purchase at: **www.PlanningShop.com**.)

MARKET SHARE DISTRIBUTION

The responses to a ComputerEase survey indicate that target companies currently conducting software training utilize providers as follows:

Current Total Market-Share Distribution for Business Software Training in Vespucci, Indiana

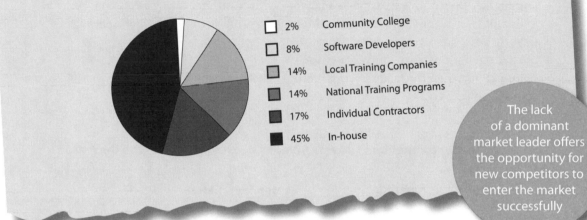

☐	2%	Community College
☐	8%	Software Developers
☐	14%	Local Training Companies
☐	14%	National Training Programs
☐	17%	Individual Contractors
■	45%	In-house

> The lack of a dominant market leader offers the opportunity for new competitors to enter the market successfully

List your major competitors (general, specific, or both). Who controls what share (portion or percentage) of the market? Are these shares increasing or decreasing? Include yourself, if you currently control part of the market. Use actual data, if available. Otherwise, estimate market-share percentage.

YOUR BUSINESS:	Market Share	Increasing or Decreasing?

COMPETITORS:	Market Share	Increasing or Decreasing?

4. Determine competitive positions

In previous worksheets, you've identified your competitors' strengths, weaknesses, and market share. Now it's time to analyze and rank your competition based on those factors. This shows you understand the relative strength of your competition and helps you focus on the factors necessary to compete effectively.

On the worksheet below, rank the specific competitors you identified on page 51 from strongest to weakest and provide reasons for their market standing.

Rank your major competitors by name from strongest to weakest. Give the reason for each ranking.

Rank	Competitor	Reason for ranking

COMPETITIVE ANALYSIS

This is how ComputerEase ranks the strengths of its competitors:

1. JMT Training
2. Seth Rose, independent
3. In-house trainers
4. National training companies
5. Other local companies
6. Online training
7. Other independent contractors

JMT is considered the strongest competitor due to its current client base, the personality and sales skills of its owner, Janice Tuffrey, and its potential to associate with national franchise training operations. However, JMT's current training staff and materials are of inconsistent quality, and current clients have expressed dissatisfaction with the lack of quality control. Moreover, JMT lacks skilled management of its financial affairs, resulting in insufficient capital for marketing and updating equipment. No other local companies have either the financial or personnel resources to adequately respond to a well-organized, sufficiently funded competitor.

Seth Rose has established a reputation as an effective trainer of spreadsheet programs and has a loyal client base. However, he has expressed a lack of interest in expanding his operation by hiring additional trainers, and he has reached full or near-full capacity. ComputerEase has begun negotiating a strategic partnership with Rose to sell additional training to his current customers. No other Independent contractor has a substantial client base or adequate resources to respond to new competition.

National training companies market their services through direct mail or telemarketers and have no local sales force. Their customer base is neither loyal nor particularly satisfied with the service.

The quality of in-house trainers varies widely. However, since these trainers are already on staff, there is little or no additional cost to the customer for using them.

Relative strengths and weaknesses highlighted

Can benefit from competitor's strengths

5. Highlight your competitive edge

Every business needs some advantages over the competition to attract customers and stay in business. In this section, present yours.

Some typical types of competitive advantages are:

- Price

- Product features

- Convenience (closer to—or faster for—customer)

- Aggressive, effective marketing program

- Choice of industries/types of customers served

- Well-known brand

- Exclusive relationships (distribution, suppliers)

- Operational efficiencies

It's also useful to show how your competitors' weaknesses become your company's strengths. Let's say the market leader in your industry is large and bureaucratic. If your company is small and nimble, explain how you are better able to respond to sudden changes in market demand. Does your competitor rely on old technology? Highlight your use of state-of-the-art tools that better serve your customers.

COMPETITIVE EDGE

ComputerEase's advantages over its competitors include:

- It's a local, as opposed to national, provider.
- It provides a local, in-person sales force solely dedicated to the corporate market.
- It offers a company-owned training center with state-of-the-art computers and up-to-date business software.
- It offers ongoing technical support for corporate clients at no or low cost.
- It has coordinated, consistent marketing and sales programs.
- Its status as an "Authorized Training Center" for major software publishers gives it credibility, joint programs, and pre-release and steeply discounted software.
- Its management is business-oriented, rather than computer-oriented.
- Its staff consists of high-quality, professional trainers, rather than contract workers.

Why will your customers choose you over your competition? List your competitive advantages.

6. Evaluate barriers to entry and potential future competition

An important factor to consider is what obstacles, if any, prevent new competition from entering the market. You may be able to take on all your current competitors, but if you're successful, will a flock of new competitors suddenly appear?

As you consider potential future competitors, think about the obstacles they might need to overcome to enter your market. Common obstacles, called "barriers to entry," include:

- Patents and trademarks

- High start-up costs

- Substantial, hard-to-find technical or industry expertise

- Market saturation

- Restrictive licensing requirements or regulations

Make a few well-founded predictions about the sources of your competition over the next five years or so. Consider:

- **New companies entering the market.** Good resources for predictions in this area include articles in industry publications or local media.

- **Existing companies expanding their product lines.** Look at companies in related fields and examine their Web sites for press releases about new product offerings. Once again, check industry media.

BARRIERS TO ENTRY AND FUTURE COMPETITION

It is relatively difficult for new competitors to enter the software training field. Substantial start-up costs are involved when purchasing or leasing equipment, and high-quality trainers are difficult to find. Moreover, software providers are becoming increasingly selective about which companies they will allow to serve as "Authorized Training Companies." These relationships are crucial in terms of receiving pre-release, below-cost copies of software, co-sponsoring product introduction events, and customer perception.

However, the long-term outlook for the industry points to nationally franchised local training companies and online "distance learning." These represent the most substantial threat. Recognizing this evolution, ComputerEase plans to affiliate with the highest-quality national franchise or independent trainers association as soon as practical and potentially add its own distance learning training.

Highlighted as a ComputerEase advantage earlier

National companies present a major threat

List your potential future competitors.

What obstacles might new competition face in trying to enter your market? What are the barriers to entry?

Pulling It All Together: The Competition

To be an effective competitor, you have to understand what you're up against. Honestly evaluating your competition, their strengths as well as their weaknesses, arms you to survive. If you think you have *no* competition, think again. If you're filling a genuine market need, then there certainly are—or will be—other companies who want a piece of the action.

Synthesize the information you've gathered into a concise, convincing description of your competition, one that highlights your competitive advantages.

What types of businesses compete with you? (See worksheet on page 47.)

_____

_____

Who are your specific competitors? (See worksheet on page 49.)

_____

_____

_____

What share (portion) of the market does each competitor control?
(See worksheet on page 51.)

_____

_____

_____

How would you rank your competitors (in terms of market position)?
(See worksheet on page 52.)

_____

_____

_____

What are your competitive advantages? (See worksheet on page 55.)

_____

_____

_____

Who will your future competitors be, and what barriers to entry do they face?
(See worksheet on page 57.)

_____

_____

_____

Accomplishments

In this step you'll:

- ☐ 1. Summarize your marketing message
- ☐ 2. Describe your marketing vehicles
- ☐ 3. Identify additional marketing and sales strategies
- ☐ 4. Describe your sales team

Time-Saving Tools

You'll complete this section more quickly if you have any of the following handy:

- ☐ Marketing collateral (brochures, advertisements, press releases)
- ☐ Marketing budget and/or expenses
- ☐ Information about your sales team
- ☐ Sales history (for an existing business)
- ☐ Sales forecasts

Step 5:
Marketing and Sales Plan

You know you have a good product or service, but can you convince customers to buy it? This is where your marketing and sales strategy comes in. It describes your plans for spreading the word about your product or service and selling to your customers.

Because your marketing and sales plan outlines your strategy for securing customers and sales, it's a critical key to your success. Investors and lenders want to see:

- A realistic, cost-effective marketing approach to informing potential customers about your products or services and the benefits offered

- An effective sales force

- Appropriate sales techniques and methods

Marketing vs. Sales

Marketing and sales, while closely related, have very different functions.

Marketing activities make customers aware of your product or service and the benefits it offers. Marketing activities include advertising (print, radio, TV, Internet), producing collateral material (brochures, product information sheets), preparing company Web sites, doing public relations (press releases, events), attending trade show exhibitions, and offering free sample giveaways.

Sales activities are direct interactions with your potential customers to solicit and procure orders or to make an immediate sale. Sales activities include in-person sales at a customer's home or place of business, telemarketing, e-commerce, direct mail, online sales, or selling merchandise in person at a store, trade show, or other event.

1. Summarize your marketing message

Every business sends a message in its marketing. To be most effective, base this message on the strategic position your company stakes out in the marketplace—the way you intend to distinguish yourself from your competitors. For instance, if you are competing on price, your message is "low-price leader." If you're competing on convenience, your message might be "one-hour service." Perhaps you are exploiting a particular niche in the market, such as "attorneys specializing in estate planning" or "software for architects."

Such messages set you apart from the competition and help customers quickly decide if you present an appropriate option for their needs and buying priorities.

Words to Sell By

Some of the best company slogans focus on their customers' needs and desires rather than their product's attributes. Here are a few examples. Be cautious, however, when attempting this approach yourself; it takes an enormous marketing budget to make these indirect taglines memorable.

SLOGAN	COMPANY	MOTIVATION
Just Do It	Nike	Customers want to reach their fitness goals
Because You're Worth It	L'Oréal	Bolsters the customer's self-image
You're in good hands with Allstate	Allstate	Customers seek security and protection
It's Everywhere You Want to Be	Visa	Customers want the convenience and financial means to live the life they desire
Live in Your World. Play in Ours.	PlayStation 2	Customers want to experience an alternative reality

MARKETING MESSAGE

ComputerEase's slogan, "We speak your language," is designed to reassure its primary market: large corporate customers. The slogan implies both that the software training itself will be comprehensible and that ComputerEase understands the needs of the business customer. As a play on the word "computerese," the name is designed to be memorable, with the added implication that the company makes dealing with computers easy.

ComputerEase prominently features its slogan, "We speak your language," on all its marketing materials, on its company Web site, and at the bottom of email messages.

Marketing message and slogan

How do you position your company in the market? How do you want customers to think of your company? Summarize your message in fifty words or less.

Do you have a company tagline or slogan? Include it here.

QUICK**TIP**

A Good Fit?

Make sure your marketing approach, and the marketing vehicles you choose, are a good fit for the type and size of business you run. A small graphic design firm may be most successful spending its marketing dollars by joining and attending local entrepreneur networking groups, while a retail store may do better advertising in a local newspaper.

2. Describe your marketing vehicles

Once you have summarized what you want to tell potential customers, explain your plan for getting your company's name and marketing message out. Will you advertise? If so, where and how often? Exhibit at trade shows? If so, at which shows and how much will that cost?

Since every marketing vehicle costs money, carefully plan how you'll spend your marketing dollars. Some options:

- Company Web site
- Product brochures
- Internet advertising
- Print media advertisements
- Broadcast media ads (radio, network and cable TV)
- Promotional items (imprinted with your company name)
- Joining networking groups
- Public relations activities
- Direct mail

On the worksheet opposite, list the types of marketing vehicles you'll use. Also, indicate how often you plan to use them and how much it will cost. You'll use these figures later, in Step 9, when you prepare your financials.

A Magazine for Fenceposts?

While the mainstream press exposes your ad to more people, highly targeted publications reach those more likely to buy. If you sell specialized fences, you'll reach more potential customers advertising in a trade journal, like *FencePost* magazine or *World Fence News*, than in a general newspaper. There are trade publications for just about every industry or interest; locate them by using an Internet search engine or check the listing of trade associations at The Planning Shop's website: **www.PlanningShop.com/tradeassocations**.

MARKETING VEHICLES

Most of ComputerEase's marketing is done through face-to-face solicitation of human resource and training directors of large corporations. To support this effort, the company has developed quality printed sales materials (brochures and class descriptions). To stay in front of this market, the company also sponsors the annual dinner of the Greater Vespucci Association of Human Resource Directors and advertises in their quarterly magazine.

Additionally, the company maintains an ongoing direct mail program. A schedule of ComputerEase's downtown classes Is sent out every two months to the target audience. Currently 3,500 pieces are sent. ComputerEase purchases lists of human resource directors and another list of local subscribers to a leading computer magazine. All prior students are also included in the direct mail program.

Marketing vehicles

What marketing vehicles will you use to deliver your message? (Advertising? Direct mail? Trade shows? Networking events?)

How frequently do you intend to use these marketing vehicles?

How much do you expect to spend on marketing each month? What is your annual marketing budget?

QUICK**TIP**

Split the Cost

If you're selling another company's products or services —or if they're selling yours— ask them to participate in co-op advertising or promotions. Since it's in both of your interests to make sales, they'll often agree to split, or share, marketing expenses. For instance, if you run a sporting goods store, a ski manufacturer may split the cost of an ad in your local newspaper promoting a sale of their product at your store.

3. Identify any additional marketing and sales strategies

In addition to traditional advertising and marketing vehicles, many businesses work with other companies to promote their businesses and make sales. Some of these strategies include:

- **Strategic Partnerships**. Associating with another company to jointly promote each other's products or services or to have them promote your company as part of their offerings.

- **Licensing Agreements**. Licensing the rights to your product or service to another company, usually enabling them to sell your product or service under their name.

- **Distribution Agreements**. Arranging with another company to market and sell your product or service for you. Distributors often have their own sales force as well as warehouse and shipping facilities.

- **Using Wholesalers**. Wholesalers buy in bulk, then divide the goods into smaller quantities to sell to many retailers.

- **Working with Agents/Brokers**. These are individuals who sell your products or services, usually on a commission basis.

MARKETING AND SALES STRATEGIES

Marketing partnerships

ComputerEase partners with leading software publishers on many collaborative marketing activities. These include sharing the cost of cooperative advertisements placed in regional computer publications, sponsoring special events to introduce corporate clients to the publishers' new software, and sponsoring a trade show booth at the regional human resource directors' annual convention.

Strategic partnerships

Additionally, ComputerEase has agreements with two local computer hardware stores and four independent computer resellers to cross-promote each other's products and services. These stores and resellers include discount coupons for ComputerEase classes with every computer purchase they make.

What other marketing and sales strategies do you use, if any? (Include tactics such as co-op advertising, third-party distribution or licensing agreements, and other strategic partnerships.)

4. Describe your sales team

Your sales team provides your most important link to your customers—and to your profits. These staff members not only sell your product/service, they also have access to critical information about your customers' needs, desires, and buying habits.

The structure of your sales force reflects your sales methods: if you rely on face-to-face sales calls, you are likely to have salespeople on staff or use independent sales representatives. If you rely on telemarketing, you may employ part-time personnel or employ an outsource telemarketing company.

On the worksheet opposite, discuss the structure of your sales force. Detail whether you use:

- Full-time personnel

- Part-time personnel

- Independent sales representatives

- Employees of a different company

Explain how you pay your salespeople. Do they get straight salary? Straight commission? Base salary and commission? What percentage commission? Describe bonuses and other incentives you provide.

Types of Sales Reps

While sales teams can take many different forms, their responsibilities generally fall into one of three categories:

Inside Sales. They make sales while on the company premises. Telemarketers and retail store sales staff are inside salespeople.

Outside Sales. They visit customers to solicit orders and often nurture ongoing professional relationships with them. Pharmaceutical company agents who visit doctors and hospitals and employees who sell products in person to key clients are all examples of outside salespeople.

Independent Sales Representatives. These are independent contractors (non-employees) who sell your products to a territory or to a range of customers. They may represent only your business; however, they often also represent products from a number of related companies at once.

SALES TEAM

Since ComputerEase's primary target market is large companies, most of its sales are made in face-to-face solicitations, primarily by the Vice President for Marketing, Susan Alexander, and also by company President Scott Connors. Both have extensive experience in selling to human resource and training directors—the primary decision makers in target companies. The average contract is projected at approximately $5,000.

The company also has two outside sales representatives on staff, each paid $20 per hour, plus commission. Their primary responsibility is marketing ComputerEase training programs to mid-size companies, a duty not handled by Alexander or Connors.

Additionally, all company personnel are considered members of the sales team. Susan Alexander is responsible for their sales training and supervision. The registrar, who takes phone registrations, is trained in phone manners and order solicitation, and she is given incentive gifts for registering targeted numbers of students for "add-on" classes. Even the software trainers themselves participate in monthly sales training meetings. All employees receive financial bonuses if the company reaches overall sales goals.

Additional motivation to make sales

Who makes sales in your company? Do you have designated salespeople? If so, how many?

How are their jobs structured? (Inside sales? Outside sales? Independent contractors?)

What are the highlights of your sales team's experience? How many combined years? Do any have a successful track record with products/services similar to yours?

How do you pay them? (Commission? Commission plus base? Salary? Bonuses? Incentives?)

How do you train them? What do you do to continually motivate them?

Pulling It All Together: Marketing and Sales Plan

To stay in business, you have to reach customers and secure sales. That is why this section of your plan is likely to be reviewed closely by prospective investors or lenders. In this section, potential funders want to see that your marketing and sales methods are appropriate for your business, and that your sales force is both large enough and well-enough trained to secure the sales levels necessary to sustain your business.

Synthesize all the marketing and sales information you've gathered into a clear, concise description of your marketing and sales plan.

What is your marketing message? (See worksheet on page 63.)

_____
_____
_____
_____

Which marketing vehicles will you use? (See worksheet on page 65.)

_____
_____
_____
_____

What other marketing and sales strategies will you employ? (See worksheet on page 67.)

_____
_____
_____
_____

Who is on your sales team, and how is it structured? (See worksheet on page 69.)

_____
_____
_____

Accomplishments

In this step you'll:

☐ 1. Describe key operational factors
☐ 2. Highlight your corporate advantage
☐ 3. Find solutions to potential problems

Time-Saving Tools

You'll complete this section more quickly if you have any of the following handy:

☐ Maps of facilities
☐ Addresses of facilities
☐ Technological diagrams
☐ Work and production flow charts
☐ Operations-related financial records

Step 6:
Operations

How are you actually going to run your business? The Operations section of your business plan briefly describes how you execute the basic functions of your company: manufacturing or creating your product or service, keeping on top of inventory, and delivering your product/service to your customer.

Emphasize any operational aspects that give your company a competitive edge. If you've found a way to cut costs, and increase profit margins, by using innovative production methods or less-expensive suppliers, highlight those aspects in your business plan.

Operational aspects of your business plan include:

- Location and facilities

- Production/manufacturing processes

- Equipment and technology

- Inventory management

- Cost controls and purchasing

- Quality control

- Customer service

How much detail you'll offer on each of these aspects depends on your type of business. For example, a catering company would focus on facilities and cost control; a limousine service would focus on equipment (vehicles) and perhaps technology (for dispatching). For more information on each of these components, see *Elements of an Operations Plan* on pages 74-75.

🔑 KEY TO SUCCESS

Your goal in this section is to show:

- You've thought through what it takes to make your company function.

- You are capable of managing those functions on a day-to-day basis.

- The reasons for any changes—and additional costs—in operations for an existing business (particularly if you're seeking funding).

Elements of an Operations Plan

- **Location and facilities.** The place you set up shop affects your ability to do business. Why did you choose this location and/or building? Proximity to your target market? Low rent or attractive lease terms? Easy access to transportation?

  How are the facilities arranged to make doing business easier? Describe the benefits of your location and facilities, *or*, if you're seeking funding to move to a new location, focus on the benefits of moving to a more appropriate place.

- **Production and quality control.** Every business has a production process. If you make a product, your process is the way you fabricate raw materials to create a new item; if yours is a service business, you'll have a method for designing and delivering your service to customers. Focus on issues such as your production methods, capacity, cost-saving procedures, and the methods you use to ensure consistent quality control.

- **Inventory control.** If you are making or selling a product, how you manage inventory levels has a direct impact on your bottom line. You can have too much money invested in inventory that is just sitting around, or, conversely, not enough inventory to fill orders. Briefly describe the ways in which you manage your inventory levels to produce the highest profits.

- **Supply and distribution.** Who do you rely on to provide you with the goods coming into your company, and who do you rely on to help sell the goods coming out? Describe the relationships you have with key suppliers or distributors and wholesalers. Are your supply channels and distribution methods reliable? Do you have long-standing relationships and/or favorable credit terms with suppliers and distributors? Highlight the relationships that give your company added stability.

- **Order fulfillment and customer service.** Once you have produced your product or planned for your service, how do you get it to your customer? What are your packaging, shipping, and warehousing systems? Do you have procedures for handling customer complaints or soliciting customer feedback? Show that you have an efficient system for fulfilling customers' orders and responding to their concerns.

- **Equipment and technology.** Perhaps you are using state-of-the art or advanced equipment and technology to run your business or produce your product. If so, discuss ways this improves operational efficiency, saves money, and/or gives you a competitive edge.

- **Financial control systems.** Do you have procedures in place to make certain that financial matters are handled promptly and accurately? How are invoices sent out? How are your bills paid? Do you have a system to ensure that key managers are regularly reviewing financial information? A system for fraud prevention?

Keep It Simple

The Operations section of your business plan is *not* intended to be an operations manual. Rather, it is a brief overview demonstrating that you understand the nitty-gritty details that make your business work.

If yours is a very small business with simple operations (a home-based graphic design firm, for instance), you can omit this section altogether. However, you should then include a paragraph or two in your Company Description outlining your basic operations, such as what technology you use.

On the other hand, if yours is a new, expanding, or complicated business, go into more detail in your Operations section. Just remember: it's not necessary—or advisable—to provide a step-by-step guide to how your company works. Save that for an operations manual you use internally.

QUICK**TIP**

Are Your Operations Socially Responsible?

Socially responsible operations often lead to an enhanced bottom line and fewer problems with government agencies. You'll impress many investors and lenders by incorporating socially responsible practices into your operations plan. Do you have methods to reduce waste and excess energy use? Do you use recycled materials in production? Do your suppliers use sustainable business practices? While social responsibility is not considered a traditional aspect of operations, it often pays to highlight those practices that show you have thought about the impact your actions have on your community and environment.

1. Determine key operations elements

In this area, highlight the most important operational aspects of your business. Review the various operational aspects described in *Elements of an Operations Plan* on pages 74-75. Focus on those most central to your company's success. You don't have to include each element in your business plan, just the ones at your company's core. A catering company, for instance, could highlight its convenient and well-equipped commercial kitchen facilities, critical for enabling the company to handle large orders.

If yours is an unusual business—or, if you are seeking funding from a source not familiar with your industry—explain enough of the basic operations to enable your readers to understand how a company like yours functions.

KEY ELEMENTS OF OPERATIONS

A key element of ComputerEase's operations is its Corporate Training Center, located at 987 South Main Street in Vespucci. The Center currently consists of twelve student computer stations, equipped with all the major business software programs, an instructor's computer station and projection equipment, and state-of-the-art technology enabling the instructor to monitor exactly what each student is doing.

The Corporate Training Center is vital because most of ComputerEase's corporate customers have limited, if any, extra computer facilities on their premises appropriate for conducting on-site corporate classes. Thus, ComputerEase can only grow to an adequate level of income by having well-equipped training facilities of its own to offer.

Describes a key operational factor

Explains reason for key factor's importance

List the operational factors most critical to your business and how you deal with them, then explain why they are important. You do not need to discuss every one of these factors here, only those key to your operations.

Your approach to:	Reason for Importance:
Location/Facilities:	
Production/Quality Control:	
Inventory Control:	
Supply/Distribution:	
Order Fulfillment/Customer Service:	
Equipment/Technology:	
Financial Control Systems:	
Other:	

2. Highlight your operational advantages

Here's where you can make your company—and your business plan—shine. Are you implementing, or devising, any operational efficiencies or innovations that give you an advantage over your competitors or increase profits? If so, be sure to highlight them here.

In this section, demonstrate how the operational choices you've made enhance your company's bottom line and give you an edge over your competition. For example, if a florist found a method of purchasing flowers directly from growers, rather than from wholesalers, he'd indicate how this improved his profit margins.

Explain any tradeoffs you've made by choosing a particular procedure, equipment or technology. The florist, for instance, might need to purchase additional refrigeration units, and incur additional costs, as a result of buying flowers directly, but could also show how those costs will be recouped in higher profits within a twelve-month period.

Which, if any, of your operational procedures or innovations enhance efficiencies, minimize costs, and/or maximize profits?

_____

_____

_____

How do these compare with other companies in your industry?

_____

_____

How do they give you a competitive edge?

_____

_____

What, if any, are the cost/benefit tradeoffs of implementing these methods?

_____

_____

_____

OPERATIONAL ADVANTAGES

Having its own training classroom enables ComputerEase to enjoy higher profit margins than its competitors.

While maintaining a classroom incurs the additional costs of rent and equipment, training classes held at ComputerEase's Corporate Training Center produce higher profit margins than classes conducted at customers' facilities ("on-site classes").

In comparison to classes held at ComputerEase's own classroom, on-site classes typically have fewer students per session, incur additional instructor and transportation costs, and increase wear and tear on equipment.

While ComputerEase charges higher fees per student for on-site classes, the market will not bear prices that truly absorb the increased costs.

Moreover, the potential customer base for Training Center classes is substantially larger than that for on-site programs. More businesses can afford to send employees to scheduled classes at ComputerEase's Corporate Training Center—or have a class developed for them at the Center—than can incur the costs and disruption of an on-site program.

ComputerEase management chose to lease rather than purchase its Corporate Training Center equipment and negotiated favorable lease terms with Wait's Computer Emporium, enabling the company to upgrade its computers every twelve months. This not only significantly reduced the initial capital outlay, which would have exceeded $50,000, but ensures that ComputerEase always has the latest technology for its students—a useful marketing, as well as educational, advantage.

With the funds now being sought, the company will open a second Corporate Training Center in the city of Abergel Peak, where many of its corporate customers are located.

Drawbacks of alternate methods

Benefits include lower costs and larger customer base

Additional advantage of state-of-the-art technology

3. Address current—or potential— operational challenges

Most companies continually face changes and challenges in their operations, such as the need to update technology or equipment, find new facilities, or implement new processes or procedures. Perhaps you're developing your business plan to raise funds to deal with these needed changes. If so, you'll need to outline the problems you're currently experiencing, or the ones you anticipate in the near future, along with how you propose to address them.

In this section, describe any operational problems and potential solutions, addressing these questions:

- What operational issues currently reduce your competitiveness or profitability?

- What operational problems do you anticipate encountering in the near future?

- How do these problems affect your ability to do business or attract customers?

- What is your current plan for overcoming these problems?

- What are the costs associated with your solutions?

Innovative Operations

Are you creating a brand-new product? If so, you may face additional operational hurdles. Is there a distribution system in place to get your goods to market? Are there adequate sources or supplies of raw materials? Have you figured out how to manufacture your product profitably?

In your business plan, briefly describe the issues facing you as an innovator and your planned solutions (without giving away trade secrets). Doing so shows that you are smart enough to realize there are added challenges when you're on the cutting edge.

OPERATIONAL CHALLENGES

Current
problem

A major part of the cost of the high-quality corporate training offered by ComputerEase comes from the training materials provided to each student. Developing, writing, and continually updating training manuals for every software program (materials are revised for each upgrade; their average lifespan is six to twelve months) costs $27 per student. To reduce waste, ComputerEase prints manuals just one day before each class begins, but doing so increases the per-unit cost.

Current
approach
to problem

The company recognized it had to substantially reduce materials costs. As new manuals are developed, they will be configured primarily for online, rather than print, delivery. All current training manuals will be available in digital form within eighteen months. This will, however, incur additional upfront costs in the development and deployment of the manuals for online access, and also require providing some tech support for students. However, making these changes will result in substantially increased profit margins within the next twelve months.

Shows
long-term
solution to
problem

What operational challenges currently face your company?

_____

_____

_____

How are you dealing with these issues?

_____

_____

_____

What operational challenges do you foresee in the future?

_____

_____

_____

How much will it cost for you to adequately address these challenges?

_____

_____

_____

Pulling It All Together: Operations

The Operations section of your business plan should not be overly detailed—save the specifics for your own internal operations manual. By describing the highlights of your operations, you show that you know how to make your company work on a day-to-day basis. This helps you to analyze any problems you're facing and think through solutions. And it increases confidence in your ability to structure and manage an efficient and profitable company.

Draw from the information you provided in the worksheets in this step to complete this final worksheet and develop the Operations section of your plan.

What are the key components of your operations structure? (See worksheet on page 77.)

_____

_____

_____

_____

In what ways do your operations structure and/or elements give you an advantage over your competition? (See worksheet on page 78.)

_____

_____

_____

_____

What are some operational challenges you're currently encountering or may face in the future? How do you plan to overcome those challenges? (See worksheet on page 81.)

_____

_____

_____

_____

Accomplishments

In this step you'll:

- ☐ 1. Highlight your key team members
- ☐ 2. Forecast future management needs
- ☐ 3. Describe your staffing structure
- ☐ 4. Identify members of your board of directors and advisory committee as well as any consultants

Time-Saving Tools

You'll complete this section more quickly if you have any of the following handy:

- ☐ Resumes of key managers
- ☐ Organizational charts
- ☐ Salary and payroll numbers
- ☐ Biographies of board members, advisors, and consultants

Step 7:
Management Structure

Many readers of your business plan will turn to the Management section first. They want to know who's running the shop. Investors and lenders want assurance that the company is managed by competent leaders. In this section, you want to show that:

- The key members of your staff are qualified to run your business.

- You understand what additional staff, if any, is necessary.

- Your staffing levels and roles are appropriate and sufficient to achieve results.

- You've turned to qualified outside advisors when necessary.

⚙ KEY TO SUCCESS
Make Your Stars Shine

Do you have any well-known, highly accomplished people associated with your company? Have any of your key personnel had experience at well-regarded companies? If so, highlight these individuals prominently in your Management section and in your Executive Summary. Well-known names increase readers' confidence in your business plan.

How you prepare this section depends on how you're going to use your business plan. If you're developing your plan to raise money, focus primarily on the backgrounds of your management team. Summarize their relevant qualifications in a concise and objective style. If, on the other hand, you are creating a plan for internal use, concentrate instead on your staffing structure and the gaps in your team.

If yours is a very small business, and you are the key—or only—employee, you can omit this section. (However, be sure to emphasize your skills and experience in your Executive Summary.) To make your business seem more substantial, add the names and credentials of key advisors, such as your attorney or accountant.

1. Highlight your key team members

This section describes the people who run your business. Develop brief summaries to explain their current roles and highlight their qualifications, past experience, education, and other characteristics, particularly as they relate to those roles. Your goal is to demonstrate you have brought together the right team to make your company successful.

Begin with the founder, usually viewed as the most important person in the company. Founders often serve as the top managers, exercising day-to-day control over business operations. Then list and briefly describe the other key members of your management team.

Some other key roles include:

- **Top decision makers:** President, chief executive officer, division president

- **Operations:** Chief operating officer, plant or production manager

- **Technology:** Chief technology officer, MIS director

- **Marketing and sales:** Vice president of marketing, director of sales

- **Human resources:** HR director, training director

(Note: Founders often fill one or more of the roles listed above.)

If you are creating a business plan primarily to seek funding, limit the number of people you include to the five or six most critical to your long-term success.

As you describe each individual, explain:

- What is their role in the company?

- What past experience or education qualifies them for the job?

- What past successes have they had?

- What are their key professional and personal strengths?

- What (if any) is their personal financial investment in the company?

KEY TEAM MEMBERS

Scott E. Connors, President. Prior to founding ComputerEase, Scott E. Connors was the regional vice president for Wait's Computer Emporium, a computer and electronics retailer with twenty-three stores in the Midwest. Before that, he was a sales representative with IBM for five years.

Connors began his association with Wait's Computer Emporium as manager of the downtown Vespucci store. In his first year, he increased sales by over 42%, in his second year by 39%. He was named "Manager of the Year" for the Wait's chain.

Connors assumed the role of regional vice president of the Wait's chain three years ago. He was responsible for the company's strategic development for Indiana, Ohio, and Illinois. In that position, Connors conducted an evaluation of the potential of adding software training to augment the chain's computer hardware sales. This evaluation led Connors to believe that a substantial need for corporate software training existed but could not be met by an electronics retailer. Instead, a stand-alone operation should be formed. This was the concept behind ComputerEase.

Connors' association with Wait's Computer Emporium, coupled with his years at IBM, has given him an extensive background selling technology services and products to large corporations.

Connors owns 60% of the stock in ComputerEase and serves as Chairman and Treasurer of the Board of Directors.

Susan Alexander, Vice President, Marketing. Susan Alexander joined ComputerEase with primary responsibility for the company's marketing and sales activities.

Prior to joining ComputerEase, Alexander served as assistant marketing director for AlwaysHere Health Care Plan. Her responsibilities included making direct sales to human resource directors, developing marketing materials and campaigns, and supervising sales personnel. She held that position for seven years prior to joining ComputerEase. Alexander's experience marketing to the human resources community gives her the ideal background for ComputerEase, which sells its services primarily through human resources and training directors.

In previous relevant positions, Alexander was a sales representative for SpeakUp Dictation Equipment, where she sold technological equipment to corporations, and copy editor for the Catchem Advertising Agency.

Alexander owns 10% of the stock in ComputerEase.

Highlights demonstrated success

Related experience

Financial commitment to the company

Experience relates to several aspects of the business

Describe the qualifications of your top-level management. List your key managers' names, job responsibilities, relevant past experience, and other noteworthy attributes.

President/CEO

_____

_____

_____

_____

Key Management: Finance/Administration

_____

_____

_____

_____

Key Management: Operations/Technology

_____

_____

_____

_____

_____

Key Management: Marketing/Sales

_____

_____

_____

_____

_____

Key Management: Human Resources/Personnel

_____

_____

_____

_____

_____

Key Management: Strategy/New Products/Research & Development

_____

_____

_____

_____

2. Predict future management needs

New or changing companies usually have not yet filled all their key management positions. If you are looking for investors or lenders, it's likely that you're going to use some of the funds raised to hire additional leaders. In this section, summarize the roles you need filled and the desired qualifications of the people you hope to bring on board. Questions to consider include:

- What roles in the company will they be filling?

- What experience, qualifications, and education (if job-related) should they have?

- What other characteristics are you looking for in these individuals?

- How will these additional managers help round out your team?

Identify the types of individuals who will round out your team. For example, if your current team has strong marketing experience but less experience in managing money, adding someone with "strong financial management experience" would be a priority in future management hires.

Use the worksheet opposite to summarize the desired qualifications of top team members you plan to hire in the next year or two. Their skills, experience, and personalities should complement those of other top managers and fill any perceived holes.

FUTURE MANAGEMENT NEEDS

Balances out other team experience

Vice President, Training (To Be Selected). In the next year, ComputerEase will add a third key management position, Vice President for Training. The individual selected will have substantial experience running a training organization, teaching others to train, and supervising a training staff. This future vice president will possess outstanding training skills and have experience with computer software programs, either in teaching or in developing such programs. Ideally, he or she will have experience in developing training manuals or other training material.

What top management positions are you seeking to fill, or will you need to fill, in the near future? Describe the roles you anticipate and qualifications you'll be looking for in any future management employees. Omit this section if you do not anticipate hiring any additional key management in the next year or two.

1. Key Management to Be Hired

2. Key Management to Be Hired

3. Key Management to Be Hired

3. Describe your staffing structure

Describe the composition of the rest of your staff, the people who carry out the day-to-day work of your company. There's no need to provide the name and qualifications of each individual. Instead, present a general summary of your staffing situation, focusing on job roles, responsibilities, and staff costs. For example, an apparel store might have three salespeople making $10 per hour, plus commission, while a restaurant might include ten part-time waiters, paid a combined $110,000 a year, plus tips.

Use the worksheet opposite to describe the makeup of your staff. Also indicate any expected changes to your staff composition or staffing levels, such as adding additional employees, or plans to outsource responsibilities to independent contractors or consultants.

Social Responsibility Leads to Healthy Bottom Lines

Social responsibility encompasses a company's treatment of its employees along with the values exemplified and communicated by the corporate culture. Do you compensate your employees fairly? Do you provide, or at least contribute to, an adequate benefits package? Is your business environment free of racism, sexism, ageism, and any other "isms" that would make it an uncomfortable place to work? While you don't need to dwell on this in your business plan, creating a fair and ethical work environment pays off. It translates into increased worker loyalty and productivity, leading to reduced turnover and training costs, as well as enhanced company image. These, in turn, can lead to greater customer loyalty and higher profits, as well as the satisfaction of knowing you've created a great place to work.

STAFF STRUCTURE

In addition to the two primary managers now on staff and a VP for Training to be hired, ComputerEase currently employs two permanent staff members. Additionally, the company contracts with training course leaders as needed, but they serve as independent contractors.

One of the two staff members serves as receptionist, customer service representative, class registrar, and mail handler. The other staff member also handles customer service, as well as dealing with tech support calls and maintaining the hardware and software for ComputerEase's classroom. Both make inside sales calls to individuals expressing interest in the company's classes (through ComputerEase's website or other leads). Each is paid $19 per hour.

As ComputerEase's course load increases, the company will hire part-time training instructors rather than relying solely on outside contractors. This will reduce costs, but as importantly, will ensure greater consistency in the quality of the company's offerings.

Staff to be hired in the future

What are the jobs of employees on your staff? List them here, along with the number of people who fill those roles, and their pay rate/range.

Job Role	Number of employees in that role	Pay Rate/Range

What staff will you add in the near future?

4. Identify your board members, advisors, and consultants

It is often a good idea—and sometimes a legal necessity—to turn outside your company for additional guidance and advice. If you have formal outside relationships, such as with the members of a board of directors, include the names and brief biographies of members in your business plan. For informal relationships, such as those with advisory committees or consultants, include information about them if they add credibility or stature to your company.

Some key outside advisors include:

Board of Directors. Boards of directors typically have legal responsibility for a company. If your company is incorporated, you're almost certainly required by law to have a board of directors. In start-ups, this may consist of only one person: the founder. In larger companies or companies with investors, the board usually consists of individuals with a financial stake in the company and, possibly, additional members knowledgeable about the industry. Venture capitalists generally require board membership as a condition of their investment.

Advisory Committee. Advisory committees do not have legal responsibility for a company. Thus, it is possible to identify a range of individuals whose ongoing expertise and advice you'd like to have for your company. Advisory committees can be very informal, and may meet infrequently, but they give you a way to ask people you respect to assist you in building your company.

Consultants and Other Professionals. Almost all new and expanding businesses rely on consultants to provide critical guidance and professional services. Include these in your plan *only* if they play a key role or if their names will add luster to your business plan. Such consultants include:

- Attorneys
- Accountants
- Management consultants
- Marketing consultants
- Industry specialists
- Technology advisors

BOARD MEMBERS, ADVISORS, AND CONSULTANTS

BOARD OF DIRECTORS
Scott E. Connors is the Chairman of the Board and Treasurer.

Cathy J. Dobbs, the company's attorney (and founder of the firm Dobbs, Kaye, and Babbitt) serves as Secretary.

The position of Vice Chairman has been reserved for an outside investor.

Board consists of founder and outside professional advisor

ADVISORY COMMITTEE
An informal advisory committee provides guidance to the officers and staff of ComputerEase. The committee meets quarterly, and members of the committee are available as resources to the company on an ongoing basis. The members represent professionals from industries directly related to ComputerEase's mission and target market.

Members of the committee:

Mary Major, Director of Human Resources, RockSolid Insurance Company

Brian Luce, Director of Training, Vespucci National Bank

Alex Arthur, Marketing Director, SANE Software

Dr. A. A. Arnold, Professor of Instructional Media, Vespucci State University

How committee serves the company

CONSULTANT
A.A. Arnold, Ph.D. Dr. A. A. Arnold, Professor of Instructional Media at Vespucci State University (VSU), serves the company as a consultant in the conception and development of training manuals. A specialist in the design of instructional materials, Dr. Arnold received his Ph.D. in Education with an emphasis on interactive computer-aided training. Currently, Dr. Arnold designs training programs for industry in addition to holding his position at VSU.

Outside consultant gives added credibility

Do you have a board of directors? If so, who are the members? List them here, along with brief biographies, including their professional expertise, financial stake, and compensation (if any).

_____

_____

If you have an advisory committee, who are the members? List them here, along with their professional affiliation, expertise, value to your company, and compensation (if any).

_____

_____

Do you use consultants? List them here, including the names of their firms, areas of expertise, and the ways in which they serve your company.

_____

_____

Pulling It All Together: Management Structure

Use the worksheet below to prepare the management section of your plan. If yours is a large company, add an organization chart to illustrate how your company is structured.

Conclusion

The success of your business depends on the people who run it. It takes capable people—with appropriate experience and abilities—to build and run a thriving company. Thus, it is no surprise that lenders and investors often turn first to the Management section of a business plan. They want to make certain the people in charge have the background necessary to manage the company.

Who are the key people on your management team? (See worksheet on page 89.)

_____

_____

_____

What management positions do you need to fill in the near future? (See worksheet on page 91.)

_____

_____

_____

What is the make up of the rest of your staff? (See worksheet on page 93.)

_____

_____

_____

Who are the members of your board of directors and advisory committee, and who are your consultants? (See worksheet on page 95.)

_____

_____

_____

8

Accomplishments

In this step you'll:

☐ 1. Define your long-term goals
☐ 2. Establish future milestones
☐ 3. Assess the risks
☐ 4. Explore exit options

Time-Saving Tools

You'll complete this section more quickly if you have any of the following handy:

☐ Existing plans for company development
☐ Calendar of planned product releases or expansion activities

Step 8:
Future Development

Since a business plan is a road map for your company, you—and those who review your plan—need a clear sense of your ultimate destination. In this section, you'll outline your long-term goals, indicating the milestones you plan to reach along the way. By developing specific objectives, you'll have signposts to measure progress as you go.

If you're seeking investors for your business, this section will be of particular interest to them. When they invest money in your company, they want to assess exactly how much they might gain eventually and how big your company might become. Only then can they understand the potential return on their investment.

It's also important, both to you and your investors, to spell out what might ultimately become of the company. How will you (and any investors) get your investments—and rewards—out of the company in the long term? Even if you're just starting your business, you'll find that considering possible exit strategies changes the way you think about your company and gives you a framework for business planning.

Finally, don't be afraid to look at the risks involved in your business. An honest assessment of risk isn't likely to frighten experienced investors or lenders. They understand that all ventures involve some risk; they'll respect the fact that you understand and anticipate the risks involved.

QUICK**TIP**

If yours is a small business, make sure your business goals fit your personal goals. If you want to be home by 4 p.m. and take long vacations, it's unrealistic to set the goal of building a very large company.

1. Define your long-term goals

What do you expect your company to look like in one year? Five years? Ten years? In this section, describe your long-term vision and plans. Be as specific as you can, focusing on issues such as:

- Sales levels

- Profit levels/margins

- Number of employees

- Number of locations

- Number of product(s)/product lines

- Market share

For example, a small accounting office might have the goal of securing twenty new corporate clients in the next year, adding two additional accountants and a bookkeeping service over the next three years, and opening a second location within the next five years.

Qualitative versus Quantitative Goals

If you have not yet determined specific, quantitative goals—the kind with numbers attached—include any other goals you have for your company. Even though these may be less specific than sales or profit goals, they still give an indication of the direction you plan for your business. Such qualitative goals include: dominating a niche market, penetrating a new market, being an industry innovator, or becoming the recognized quality leader.

LONG-TERM GOALS

ComputerEase plans to grow steadily over the next five years, becoming the premier provider of software training to large- and medium-sized businesses in the Greater Vespucci region. It will capture a market share of at least 50% of all corporate software training (in terms of revenues) in the area. Within ten years, the company plans to have expanded throughout the Midwest, with offices in five to ten locations, having captured at least one-third of the share of the corporate software training market in the region.

> Intends to become a local market leader

Describe what your company will look like in the future. Be specific about sales levels, products, profit levels, and numbers of employees and locations.

What are the specific goals you have for your company in the next year?

What will your company achieve in the next three to five years?

What will your business look like in ten years?

QUICK**TIP**

One Thing at a Time

Most entrepreneurs have many good—even great—ideas on how to grow their businesses. But it's easy to get distracted by too many good ideas. Focus on building one aspect of your business at a time. Demonstrate that you can plan, execute, and succeed in one stage of your business before moving on to the next.

2. Establish future milestones

How will you know that you are making progress toward your long-term goals? Milestones will help you measure how far you've come.

Your milestones should be described in specific numerical terms so you'll know if you're making sufficient progress toward your goals. The accounting office, for instance, could set as a future milestone reaching $650,000 in revenue by the end of the second year, or have a goal of adding five new clients within the next three years.

Outlining your milestones also serves as a step-by-step guide, showing how you intend to carry out your long-term business development plans. If, for instance, your goal is to reach sales of $3 million by year five, indicate how much you'll need in sales by years two, three, and four. Then, indicate the strategies you'll use to get to those levels. Will you add marketing staff? Start a direct mail campaign? Add locations or product lines?

A milestone list allows you and your investors to see what you plan to accomplish, and it sets out clear objectives. These objectives are an essential part of your business plan.

What Milestones Have You Reached?

Instill confidence in your future prospects by highlighting your past achievements, the milestones you've already reached with your business. Include these past milestones in your Company Description (see page 19). But don't be afraid to repeat them here if they demonstrate that you're likely to reach your future goals, as well. For example, if you've already established strategic partnerships with three industry leaders, that's a good indication you can forge three more as you've indicated in your future milestone list.

FUTURE MILESTONES AND DEVELOPMENT STRATEGY

To reach the long-term goal of becoming one of the dominant companies in corporate software training in the Midwest, ComputerEase will add training classrooms and locations each year for the next three years.

First year milestone

The first priority is to open the company's second Corporate Training Center in the city of Abergel Peak within a year. Many large- and medium-sized businesses are located in the immediate vicinity of Abergel Peak, and the location can serve both as an additional training classroom and as a base of additional marketing activities. One new full-time marketing employee will be added to work out of that location.

In each of the following two years, ComputerEase plans on opening at least one additional company-run Corporate Training Center, concentrating on cities within a three-hour drive of Vespucci that have a substantial number of large- and medium-sized corporations.

Describes short-term strategies necessary to meet longer-term goals

Additionally, within twenty-four months, ComputerEase will launch its online training program. To do so, a consulting firm specializing in the development of such online training programming must be hired within the next six to nine months.

By year three, ComputerEase management will assess future options for growth. Likely scenarios include the addition of more company-run Corporate Training Centers or the possibility of franchising the operation.

Long-term expansion strategies

List the specific accomplishments you'll achieve on the way to your long-term goals. Give numerical objectives—sales and profit figures, number of customers, employees, and locations—and target dates.

Milestone	Level Achieved	Target Date

What specific steps will you take to reach those milestones?

3. Assess the risks

Running a business entails a measure of risk. Even a company with highly qualified management and well-conceived strategies might be affected by outside events.

Some types of risk any company—including yours—faces include:

- **Competitive risk.** Competitors may drive down prices, market their product or service more aggressively, or substantially enhance their offerings; new competitors may enter the field.

- **Market risk.** The economic health, needs, or desires of the target market may change.

- **Operational risk.** Critical aspects of your operations may change—suppliers may go out of business; equipment or technology may change.

- **Financial risk.** The cost of materials, energy, or labor may rise substantially.

- **Execution risk.** You may not be able to achieve the results planned in the time predicted, or you may not be able to manage your growth.

- **Economic risk.** The health of the overall economy may change, or specific financial factors, such as interest rates, may have a negative effect.

In this section, spell out the risks you're most likely to face, along with the steps you'll take to reduce those risks. If you're looking for funding, show investors or lenders that you're realistic about the challenges you could face.

RISK ASSESSMENT

Identifies risks from potential competition

The biggest risk facing ComputerEase is from new competitors entering the market from outside the Greater Vespucci area. It is highly likely that existing franchised software training companies from other parts of the country will open franchises in this region. Since these national companies offer financing to their franchisees, the major barrier to entry—the cost of establishing a training center—can be overcome. If the franchisee is highly capable, this represents the greatest risk to ComputerEase.

To prepare for this eventuality, it is critical that ComputerEase quickly and aggressively increase its market share in the region. Corporate customers are slow to change established vendors, and the company anticipates that they will be able to retain a high percentage of existing customers even in the face of new competitors. Moreover, ComputerEase management remains open to the possibility of a merger or other agreement with a national company if that appears to be a better financial option.

Strategy for reducing risk

The second-greatest risk is that significant changes will occur in the market. ComputerEase is highly dependent on the corporate market. Companies leaving the area, downsizing, or reducing their training budget would have a direct negative effect on ComputerEase revenues.

To counteract this, the company will increase its marketing of Saturday classes—and add evening classes—for consumers. In the event of layoffs, individuals will need to take classes to improve their skills, and this will provide some balance to the corporate market.

What are the potential risks facing your company? List them here, along with your plans to minimize them.

Potential Risk	Plan to Reduce Risk

4. Explore exit strategies

If you're just starting your business, it's hard to imagine what might eventually become of your company. But thinking through scenarios of what might ultimately happen to your business is helpful to you, and it's absolutely essential for investors.

An exit strategy gives focus to how you'll build your business. If you'd eventually like to sell your business, you're going to plan your business quite differently than if you'd like to hand it down to your children or have it go public on a stock exchange. See page 108 for more on exit plans.

If there's more than one partner or principal in the business, having a clear exit strategy reduces the friction that can come from having unspoken assumptions. One founder may dream of building a company worth millions and selling it in a few years, while the other may hope to build a modest company they can run together for many years. Sitting down and clarifying an exit strategy puts both on the same track.

An exit plan is absolutely critical if you're looking for investors. After all, they want to know how they will get their money back. Once you've built up the value of your business, how will that value be converted to cash or easily traded stock?

THE EXIT PLAN

By establishing itself as a regional market leader, ComputerEase will become a likely target for acquisition by a national software training company or other national for-profit educational institution. For-profit education companies are among the fastest growing firms in the U.S., and they regularly acquire existing training schools as a method of achieving their growth.

Moreover, as other software training companies have demonstrated, the ComputerEase concept lends itself well to franchising. Franchising would produce additional revenue streams to the company from the franchisees, both from franchise fees and through the purchase of materials and staff training. If the decision is made to franchise, venture capital investment will be sought. Current investors could choose to liquidate their holdings in ComputerEase at that time or convert their holdings to stock in the franchise operation.

Describe the likely exit strategies for your company. If you're seeking investors, concentrate on strategies enabling you and investors to convert the value of your company to cash or easily traded stock.

Exit Plan Options

OPTION	DESCRIPTION	BENEFITS	DRAWBACKS
Go public	Sell stock in the company on a public stock exchange	The stock easily converts to cash; liquidity	Must be a large company; approx. $25 to $50 million; highly regulated
Acquisition	Another company buys yours	Investors receive cash and/or stock	Must be a good fit for the existing company; company must have clear value
Sale	Individuals buy the company	Investors get cash	Must find a willing buyer; company must have clear value
Merger	Join with an existing company	Investors may receive stock in the new company or some cash	Usually little or no cash; stock may not be easily traded
Buy-Out	One or more current shareholders buy out the interest of another	Sellers get cash	Buyer must have sufficient cash; negotiations often contentious
Franchise	Replicate concept by licensing rights to others	Receive cash; franchisees finance expansion	Concept must be appropriate; legally complicated
Hand-Down	Give company to the next generation	Stays in family	Family tensions; little or no cash; tax implications
Close	End operations	Relatively easy; sense of closure	No financial reward; possible sense of loss

What Is ROI?

One of the most important factors investors consider when deciding whether to finance a company is the potential ROI, or Return on Investment.

ROI is the amount of money an investor gains in return for their investment. ROI is usually expressed as an annual percentage of the total investment. This figure makes it possible to quickly compare different financial opportunities, such as investing in a specific company versus investing in the stock market. Investors are looking for the largest return on their money, so the higher the ROI, the better.

The basic factors determining an investment's ROI include:

* All financial costs—initial investment and any follow-on investments

* All financial gains—including both the increase in funds (if any) from the investment and the return of the investors' money

* Time period—how long it takes to realize these gains

There may also be non-financial benefits of an investment that figure in an investor's decision, such as the satisfaction to be gained from participating in a young company's growth.

Let's say an investor is considering investing in one of two companies:

* Company A: A $50,000 investment is projected to return a total of $100,000 to the investor in 2 years.

* Company B: A $150,000 investment is projected to return a total of $300,000 to the investor in 4 years.

In both scenarios, the investor doubles their money. So which is the better investment?

An investment in Company B nets the investor a larger monetary gain: $150,000 versus only $50,000 in Company A. *But*, due to the length of time required before the investment in Company B pays off, the simple ROI in Company A is actually higher:

* Company A: 200% return in 2 years or 100% ROI per year

* Company B: 200% return in 4 years or 50% ROI per year

Pulling It All Together: Future Development

The Development section of your business plan shows you have given careful thought to how your business will grow over time. Present your readers with a clear vision of your future, along with a realistic strategy for getting there. Be sure your plan incorporates well-defined goals, specific milestones, and an honest assessment of risk. And be certain to include an exit plan; demonstrate how you and your investors can eventually recover the investment you've put into your company and convert any increase in value into cash.

What is your long-term goal for your company's future? (See worksheet on page 101.)

What milestones will you reach along the way? (See worksheet on page 103.)

What are the risks involved and how will you minimize those risks? (See worksheet on page 105.)

What are possible exit options? (See worksheet on page 107.)

9

STEP 9: **Financials**

Accomplishments

In this step you'll:

- ☐ 1. Produce your Income Statement
- ☐ 2. Develop your Cash-Flow Projection
- ☐ 3. Generate your Balance Sheet
- ☐ 4. Show your Sources and Use of Funds
- ☐ 5. Consider preparing additional supporting financial statements

Time-Saving Tools

You'll complete this section more quickly if you have any of the following handy:

- ☐ Current and past financial records
- ☐ Historical sales figures
- ☐ Projected costs
- ☐ Payroll numbers
- ☐ Any past loan documents
- ☐ Company tax returns for past years (for an existing company)
- ☐ Sales projections, marketing budget, staffing budget

Step 9:
Financials

People in business fall into one of two categories: those who fear dealing with numbers and those who are fascinated by them. If you're in the first category, the prospect of completing all your financial statements can be intimidating.

Moreover, if you're using your business plan to seek funding, it's daunting to know that investors or lenders often turn to the financials first. That's because your financials give a clear picture of how you earn and spend your money and how big you expect your company to become.

Take heart: numbers are not magical, mysterious, or menacing. They merely reflect the decisions you've made in planning or running your business. If you run ads every week in your local newspaper, there's a number associated with that. If you hire a person to help with shipping, there's a number associated with that, too.

Of course, if yours is an existing—rather than a new—company, you may already have many of these financial documents, or the basis for creating them. Examine your past financial performance and expenses when putting together your future projections and include historical numbers in your business plan.

🔑 KEY TO SUCCESS

Overcoming Finance-Phobia

If you shy away from dealing with numbers, it's easy to get into financial trouble. Learn to pay attention to your ongoing financial situation. It will help you avoid unpleasant surprises. Even if you leave the number-crunching, bill paying, and financial data entry to someone else, familiarize yourself with how to read and understand your financial statements. They'll help you make better business decisions and retain more control over your operations.

The Most Important Financial Statements

The four most important financial statements to include in your business plan are:

1. **Income Statement.** Shows whether your business is profitable (this is also called a Profit & Loss statement or "P&L").

2. **Cash-Flow Projection.** Indicates whether you'll have enough money to pay your bills.

3. **Balance Sheet.** Shows the value of your company—your total assets and liabilities.

And, if you're seeking financing:

4. **Sources and Use of Funds.** Explains where the money you need to run your business will come from (including your own pocket) and the major ways you intend to use it.

These four financial statements act as a summary of your entire financial picture, and they may be the only financial statements you need to include with your business plan, especially if yours is a simple business.

However, before preparing these four major financial statements, you'll find it helpful to produce the following:

- **Sales Projections**. Estimates your levels of sales and revenues in specific time periods.

- **Marketing Budget:** Details how much money you'll spend on all your marketing activities: advertising, trade shows, sales materials, and so on.

- **Staffing Budget:** Outlines your staffing levels, staff positions, and costs.

See page 138 for more information.

Time Periods to Cover

Some investors or lenders will tell you the time periods they want your financial statements to cover. If not, here are typical guidelines for:

New businesses: One to three years. First year, monthly projections; years two and three, quarterly projections.

Existing businesses: Same as for new businesses *plus* historical financial records from the past three to five years.

Businesses seeking venture capital: Five-year projections. First one to two years, monthly; years two and three, quarterly; years four and five, annual projections.

Additional Financials

Depending on the nature of your business (and the demands of your investors or lenders), there are a number of additional financial documents you can choose to include with your business plan. These include:

- **Break-Even Analysis.** Calculates how much you need to make in sales each month before you begin to make a profit.

- **Capital Expenditures.** Details purchases of tangible property, such as facilities, land, equipment, vehicles, and computers. Such purchases have different tax and accounting implications than other expenses.

- **Inventory.** Details the amount you spend or have tied up in inventory.

- **Professional Services Budget.** For a company that depends heavily on outsourced professionals, including independent contractors, consultants, attorneys, and accountants.

Since most businesses do not need to include these financial statements with their business plans, they are not included here. However templates for these (and additional financial statements) are included in the Electronic Financial Worksheets available for download purchase at The Planning Shop: *www.PlanningShop.com*

QUICK**TIP**

Hire a Professional

Every business benefits by having access to the services of an accountant or bookkeeper, especially in the early stages. Among their many valuable services, they'll help:

- Set up your books

- Assist you in understanding financial terms and legal requirements

- Provide valuable advice on billing, payment, and payroll procedures

- Advise you on tax-saving strategies

- Assist with the financial components of your business plan

1. Produce your Income Statement

Your Income Statement, also referred to as a Profit and Loss (P&L) statement, is the most widely relied upon of your financial statements. It summarizes the amount of money taken in and the amount of money spent over a designated period of time. This summary of revenue and expenditures reveals whether your company is profitable. It is read from top to bottom, with the first line showing total overall sales. Each subsequent line shows expenses that are deducted from your income until you get to the number at the end representing your profit or loss: your "bottom line."

To prepare your Income Statement, gather detailed information about your sales and expenses. Feel free to change the terms/language on the specific lines—especially in the expenses section—to mirror the categories you use to maintain your own accounts. Using the worksheet on pages 122–123, compile your pro forma (projected) Income Statements on a month-by-month basis. Use the same line items to produce annual or quarterly Income Statements. If yours is an existing business, use the same form for your historical Income Statements.

Your Income Statement provides the quickest overview of your company's profitability. Investors and lenders are naturally interested to know when you're going to be profitable and how much money you'll be making.

In addition to a month-by-month Income Statement for the current or coming year, include projections for the next few years. On the pages that follow are two sample Income Statements: a month-by-month Income Statement for the fictional company ComputerEase's first year in business (pages 118–119) and a three-year projection compiled on an annual basis (page 120).

Income Statement Terms

Additional terms are defined in the *Business Terms Glossary* included on pages 170–171.

- **Gross Sales**: Total sales from all product line categories before *any* costs.

- **Allowances**: Amounts deducted from invoices for reasons such as buyer's speedy payment, large quantity purchases, or acceptance of faulty merchandise.

- **Net Sales**: Amount of total sales after deducting sales commissions, returns, and allowances.

- **Cost of Goods (COG):** Costs of raw materials, inventory, or other expenses directly associated with producing the product/service for sale.

- **Gross Profit:** Amount of sales after deducting commissions, returns, allowances, and cost of goods.

- **Depreciation**: Not a cash expenditure, but the amount allowed for tax purposes for the cost of ongoing wear-and-tear of fixed assets (facilities and equipment).

- **Net Income**: Amount of income after deducting all costs of doing business.

- **Net Profit**: Amount of income after deducting all costs *plus* taxes.

QUICK**TIP**

Measuring Profitability

While an Income Statement is a reflection of a company's profit, it doesn't present the complete financial picture. For example, a business that's losing money on an annual basis could still be worth quite a lot because it owns valuable property—that will show up on the Balance Sheet. On the other hand, a profitable company may not have the cash flow to pay the bills. An Income Statement doesn't reveal either of these conditions.

INCOME STATEMENT

Year: 2006 (Actual through 8/31/06, projected 9-12/06)

	Jan	Feb	Mar	Apr	May
Income					
Gross Sales	$0	$2,000	$2,000	$5,000	$12,000
(Sales commissions)	0	0	0	0	350
(Returns and allowances)	0	0	0	0	0
Net Sales	0	2,000	2,000	5,000	11,650
(Cost of Goods)	0	324	324	812	1,946
GROSS PROFIT	0	1,676	1,676	4,188	9,704
OPERATING EXPENSES					
General and Administrative Expenses					
Salaries and wages	2,500	3,700	5,700	6,200	7,700
Employee benefits	275	275	510	510	510
Payroll taxes	210	310	505	505	505
Professional services	2,500	250	2,000	200	200
Rent	0	0	0	0	0
Maintenance	0	0	0	0	0
Equipment rental	250	250	250	250	250
Furniture and equipment purchase	0	0	0	410	0
Depreciation and amortization	2,000	0	0	0	0
Insurance	400	0	0	200	0
Interest expenses	0	125	125	125	125
Utilities	250	60	125	210	160
Telephone service	100	50	100	100	120
Office supplies	450	125	215	185	125
Postage and shipping	210	80	310	65	450
Marketing and advertising	3,200	1,800	4,000	1,500	1,500
Travel	55	150	100	150	0
Entertainment	0	0	110	320	195
Technology	3,000	0	0	0	0
TOTAL OPERATING EXPENSES	15,400	7,175	14,050	10,930	11,840
Net Income before taxes	(15,400)	(5,499)	(12,374)	(6,742)	(2,136)
Taxes on income	0	0	0	0	0
NET PROFIT AFTER TAXES	(15,400)	(5,499)	(12,374)	(6,742)	(2,136)

June	July	Aug	Sep	Oct	Nov	Dec	TOTAL
$16,000	**$20,500**	**$28,000**	**$34,200**	**$41,800**	**$50,000**	**$21,500**	**$233,000**
750	775	1,235	1,500	1,850	2,200	950	**$9,610**
0	0	0	0	0	0	0	**$0**
15,250	**19,725**	**26,765**	**32,700**	**39,950**	**47,800**	**20,550**	**$223,390**
2,595	3,449	4,741	5,691	6,926	8,400	3,662	**$38,870**
12,655	**16,276**	**22,024**	**27,009**	**33,024**	**39,400**	**16,888**	**$184,520**
8,400	6,300	9,900	9,100	10,100	11,100	8,300	**$89,000**
510	510	700	700	700	700	700	**$6,600**
505	505	610	610	610	610	610	**$6,095**
200	200	1,200	200	200	200	200	**$7,550**
0	0	2,100	2,100	2,100	2,100	2,100	**$10,500**
0	0	120	120	120	120	120	**$600**
250	250	2,000	2,000	2,000	2,000	2,000	**$11,750**
0	0	0	0	0	0	0	**$410**
0	0	0	0	0	0	0	**$2,000**
0	200	1,000	350	550	350	350	**$3,400**
125	125	125	125	125	125	125	**$1,375**
200	175	260	220	210	180	150	**$2,200**
130	100	250	200	200	200	200	**$1,750**
85	110	1,100	250	250	250	250	**$3,395**
85	260	60	410	75	300	200	**$2,505**
300	1,500	1,750	2,000	250	2,000	250	**$20,050**
25	100	0	150	150	150	150	**$1,180**
200	75	85	50	50	50	50	**$1,185**
3,000	0	0	0	0	0	0	**$6,000**
14,015	**10,410**	**21,260**	**18,585**	**17,690**	**20,435**	**15,755**	**$177,545**
(1,360)	**5,866**	**764**	**8,424**	**15,334**	**18,965**	**1,133**	**$6,975**
0	0	0	0	0	0	1,046	**$1,046**
(1,360)	**5,866**	**764**	**8,424**	**15,334**	**18,965**	**87**	**$5,929**

INCOME STATEMENT—THREE-YEAR PROJECTION

	2006	2007	2008
Income			
Gross Sales	**$233,000**	**$493,875**	**$818,615**
(Commissions)	9,610	61,360	82,920
(Returns and allowances)	0	0	0
Net Sales	**223,390**	**432,515**	**735,695**
(Cost of goods)	38,870	62,133	86,610
GROSS PROFIT	**184,520**	**370,382**	**649,085**
OPERATING EXPENSES			
General and Administrative Expenses			
Salaries and wages	89,000	176,800	226,600
Employee benefits	6,600	15,000	21,600
Payroll taxes	6,095	15,000	20,000
Professional services	7,550	5,000	6,000
Rent	10,500	39,000	39,000
Maintenance	600	3,000	4,500
Equipment rental	11,750	38,000	48,000
Furniture and equipment purchase	410	500	0
Depreciation and amortization	2,000	4,000	4,000
Insurance	3,400	4,200	5,500
Interest expenses	1,375	1,500	0
Utilities	2,200	5,000	5,500
Telephone service	1,750	1,200	2,000
Office supplies	3,395	5,000	6,000
Postage and shipping	2,505	3,600	5,000
Marketing and advertising	20,050	30,000	45,000
Travel	1,180	2,595	4,570
Entertainment	1,185	1,805	3,430
Technology	6,000	10,000	14,000
TOTAL OPERATING EXPENSES	**177,545**	**361,200**	**460,700**
Net Income before taxes	**6,975**	**9,182**	**188,385**
Provision for taxes on income	1,046	1,377	56,720
NET INCOME AFTER TAXES	**5,929**	**7,805**	**131,665**

INCOME STATEMENT					
	January	February	March	April	May
For Year _____					
INCOME					
Gross Sales					
(Commissions)					
(Returns and allowances)					
Net Sales					
(Cost of Goods)					
GROSS PROFIT					
OPERATING EXPENSES					
General and Administrative Expenses					
Salaries and wages					
Employee benefits					
Payroll taxes					
Professional services					
Marketing and advertising					
Rent					
Equipment rental					
Maintenance					
Depreciation					
Insurance					
Telephone service					
Utilities					
Office supplies					
Postage and shipping					
Travel					
Entertainment					
Interest on loans					
Other:					
Other:					
TOTAL OPERATING EXPENSES					
Net income before taxes					
Provision for taxes on income					
NET PROFIT AFTER TAXES					

June	July	August	September	October	November	December	TOTAL

2. Develop your Cash-Flow Projection

On a day-to-day basis, your Cash-Flow Projection is your most important financial analysis. It shows how much money you have coming into your business and how much going out. This "flow" indicates whether you'll have enough cash to pay your bills.

The Cash-Flow Projection is not about profit—that shows up on the Income Statement. And it's not about the overall value of your company—that appears on the Balance Sheet. It's about how much money you have in the bank. It's a real-life picture of your cash situation.

Cash-Flow Projections are particularly important for seasonal businesses, those with large inventories, and businesses that sell primarily on credit. You must plan for the lag time between buying materials, making sales, and actually receiving cash.

In preparing Cash-Flow Projections, existing businesses should review past financial records to determine actual income and expense patterns. New businesses can check with others in their industry to gauge typical payment patterns.

The Cash Crunch

Even profitable businesses can easily get into a cash crunch, so keep an eye on your bank balance. Many businesses—especially growing companies—spend more than they receive on a month-by-month basis. After all, you typically have to pay for raw materials months before you're going to receive payment for the finished product. This delay presents a tricky problem for entrepreneurs, and most businesses use lines of credit or other financing tools to manage their cash-flow needs.

Cash-Flow Terms

- **Cash Sales:** Sales made where the income is received immediately. These can include credit card sales because the revenue is deposited in the company's bank within days.

- **Collections:** Income collected from accounts receivable—sales made on credit in a previous period.

- **Interest Income:** Cash received from interest-bearing accounts, such as certificates of deposit or interest on accounts receivable.

- **Loan Proceeds:** Cash received as a result of taking out a loan, credit card advance, or other credit line.

- **Equity Capital Investments:** Cash received from investors in return for a share of ownership (equity).

- **Owner's Draw:** Money paid to owner instead of (or in addition to) a salary.

- **Opening Cash Balance:** The amount of money in the bank or account at the beginning of the period (month/year/quarter)—the same as the previous period's Ending Cash Balance.

CASH-FLOW PROJECTION

Year: 2006

	Jan	Feb	Mar	Apr	May
CASH RECEIPTS					
Income from Sales					
Cash sales	$0	$2,000	$2,000	$5,000	$12,000
Collections	0	0	0	0	0
Total Cash from Sales	**0**	**2,000**	**2,000**	**5,000**	**12,000**
Income from Financing					
Interest income	0	0	0	0	0
Loan proceeds	15,000	0	0	6,000	10,000
Equity Capital Investments	20,000	0	10,000	0	0
Total Cash from Financing	**35,000**	**0**	**10,000**	**6,000**	**10,000**
Total Cash Receipts	**35,000**	**2,000**	**12,000**	**11,000**	**22,000**
CASH DISBURSEMENTS					
Expenses					
Cost of goods	0	324	324	812	1,946
Operating expenses	15,400	7,175	14,050	10,930	11,840
Commissions/returns & allowances	0	0	0	0	350
Loan payments	0	125	125	125	125
Income tax payments	0	0	0	0	0
Other expenses/equip purchase	10,000	0	0	0	0
Reserve	0	0	0	0	0
Owner's draw	0	0	0	0	0
Total Cash Disbursements	**25,400**	**7,624**	**14,499**	**11,867**	**14,261**
Net Cash Flow	**9,600**	**(5,624)**	**(2,499)**	**(867)**	**7,739**
Opening Cash balance	**0**	**9,600**	**3,976**	**1,477**	**610**
Cash receipts	35,000	2,000	12,000	11,000	22,000
Cash disbursements	(25,400)	(7,624)	(14,499)	(11,867)	(14,261)
Ending Cash Balance	**9,600**	**3,976**	**1,477**	**610**	**8,349**

June	July	Aug	Sep	Oct	Nov	Dec	TOTAL
$12,000	15,500	19,800	20,000	30,800	35,000	15,500	**$169,600**
4,000	5,000	8,200	14,200	11,000	15,000	6,000	**$63,400**
16,000	**20,500**	**28,000**	**34,200**	**41,800**	**50,000**	**21,500**	**$233,000**
0	0	0	0	0	0	0	**$0**
0	0	4,000	0	0	0	0	**$35,000**
0	0	0	0	0	0	0	**$30,000**
0	**0**	**4,000**	**0**	**0**	**0**	**0**	**$65,000**
16,000	**20,500**	**32,000**	**34,200**	**41,800**	**50,000**	**21,500**	**$298,000**
2,595	3,449	4,741	5,691	6,926	8,400	3,662	**$38,870**
14,015	10,410	21,260	18,585	17,690	20,435	15,755	**$177,545**
750	775	1,235	1,500	1,850	2,200	950	**$9,610**
125	125	125	125	125	5,125	10,125	**$16,375**
0	0	0	0	0	0	0	**$0**
0	0	0	0	0	0	0	**$10,000**
0	0	0	0	0	5,000	5,000	**$10,000**
0	0	0	0	0	0	0	**$0**
17,485	**14,759**	**27,361**	**25,901**	**26,591**	**41,160**	**35,492**	**$262,400**
(1,485)	**5,741**	**4,639**	**8,299**	**15,209**	**8,840**	**(13,992)**	**$35,600**
8,349	**6,864**	**12,605**	**17,244**	**25,543**	**40,752**	**49,592**	**$0**
16,000	20,500	32,000	34,200	41,800	50,000	21,500	**$298,000**
(17,485)	(14,759)	(27,361)	(25,901)	(26,591)	(41,160)	(35,492)	**($262,400)**
6,864	**12,605**	**17,244**	**25,543**	**40,752**	**49,592**	**35,600**	

CASH-FLOW PROJECTION

	January	February	March	April	May
For Year _____					
CASH RECEIPTS					
Income from Sales					
Cash Sales					
Collections					
Total Cash from Sales					
Income from Financing					
Interest Income					
Loan Proceeds					
Equity Capital Investments					
Total Cash from Financing					
Other Cash Receipts					
TOTAL CASH RECEIPTS					
CASH DISBURSEMENTS					
Inventory					
Operating Expenses					
Commissions/Returns & Allowances					
Capital Purchases					
Loan Payments					
Income Tax Payments					
Investor Dividend Payments					
Owner's Draw					
TOTAL CASH DISBURSEMENTS					
NET CASH FLOW					
Opening Cash Balance					
Cash Receipts					
Cash Disbursements					
ENDING CASH BALANCE					

	CASH-FLOW PROJECTION						
June	**July**	**August**	**September**	**October**	**November**	**December**	**TOTAL**

3. Generate your Balance Sheet

If you're new to business, the Balance Sheet is likely the most perplexing of the major financial statements. It measures the overall value of your company at a particular time, but this can seem far less tangible than your profits (seen in your Income Statement) or actual cash (appearing in your Cash-Flow Projection).

The Balance Sheet itself is divided into two parts:

- The top part, where you list all your assets, such as cash, inventory, real estate, equipment, vehicles, and accounts receivable.

- The bottom part, where you total your liabilities, including accounts payable, loans, and payroll. The remaining amount (if any) is figured to be the *net worth*, expressed as shareholders' equity or retained earnings.

The final amounts for each part should be exactly equal—or *balance.*

The Balance Sheet presents investors and lenders with a snapshot of how much your company is worth, especially if it had to be sold. It shows the value of all tangible property and the extent of all debt. The value of some companies' assets may far exceed their profits, while other companies may show a profit but have heavy long-term debt.

Balance-Sheet Terms

- **Current Assets:** Anything your company has that can be turned into cash relatively quickly, including accounts receivable, inventory, and cash itself.

- **Fixed Assets:** Any tangible property your company owns that could be turned into cash more slowly, including real estate, equipment, and vehicles.

- **Current Liabilities:** Any accounts payable or other bills, debts, or financial obligations that must be paid relatively soon.

- **Long Term Liabilities:** Any financial obligations that must be paid over time, such as mortgages, loans, and equipment loans.

- **Net Worth:** The value of the company after deducting all liabilities from all assets.

- **Paid-In Capital:** Capital received from investors, as opposed to capital generated by the operations of a company.

BALANCE SHEET

For ComputerEase, Inc.

For Year Ending: December 31, 2006

ASSETS

Current Assets

Cash	$35,600	
Accounts Receivable	17,200	
Inventory	2,100	
Prepaid expenses	780	
Total Current Assets		**$55,680**

Fixed Assets

Land	0	
Buildings	0	
Furniture / equipment	10,000	
Less Accumulated Depreciation	(2,000)	
Total Fixed Assets		**$8,000**
Other Assets		0
TOTAL ASSETS		**$63,680**

LIABILITIES

Current Liabilities

Accounts Payable	8,675	
Accrued Payroll	3,050	
Taxes Payable	295	
Short-Term Notes Payable	5,000	
Total Current Liabilities		**$17,020**

Long-Term Liabilities

Long-Term Notes Payable	15,000	
Total Long-Term Liabilities		**$15,000**

Net Worth

Paid-In Capital	31,660	
Retained earnings	0	
Total Net Worth		**$31,660**
TOTAL LIABILITIES AND NET WORTH		**$63,680**

BALANCE SHEET

Your Company Name

Quarter _____ Year _____

ASSETS

Current Assets

Cash _____

Accounts Receivable _____

Inventory _____

Other Current Assets _____

Total Current Assets _____

Fixed Assets

Land _____

Facilities _____

Equipment _____

Computers & Telecommunications _____

(Less Accumulated Depreciation) _____

Total Fixed Assets _____

Other Assets _____

TOTAL ASSETS _____

LIABILITIES

Current Liabilities

Accounts Payable _____

Accrued Payroll _____

Taxes Payable _____

Short-Term Notes Payable _____

Total Current Liabilities _____

Long-Term Liabilities

Long-Term Notes Payable _____

Other Long-Term Liabilities _____

Total Long-Term Liabilities _____

NET WORTH

Paid-In Capital _____

Retained Earnings _____

Total Net Worth _____

TOTAL LIABILITIES AND NET WORTH _____

Accentuate Growth

Financing sources generally prefer to fund companies that are planning to use their newly acquired money for growth rather than to pay off old bills. After all, if you're in financial hot water now, what's to keep you from getting in trouble again? They also like to know they're not the only ones who believe in your business. So, if you can, it's important to:

• Demonstrate you are using funds to start or expand a business

• Indicate you already have commitment from other respected sources

• Show that the owners are committing their own funds as well

4. Show your Sources and Use of Funds

If you are seeking outside financing—loans or investments—you'll need to prepare one more key financial document: the Sources and Use of Funds statement. Your financing sources naturally want to know how much money you need, where you plan to get it, and what you're going to do with the money you raise. They also want to see if you've contributed any of your own money.

The Sources and Use of Funds statement can be a relatively simple one-page (or less) listing. Your task here is to assure investors and lenders that:

• You have specific plans for the money you raise

• They are aware of all the sources of funds you're seeking or have received

• You are not thoughtlessly taking on debt or giving up equity

• Ideally, you are using the money to help your business grow

Sources and Use of Funds Terms

- **Equity Financing:** Money raised from investors who receive a share of the company's ownership in return for their funds.

- **Debt Financing:** Money raised by taking on loans, leases, mortgages, or other financial obligations. Funders receive additional interest payments as well as return of their initial capital in exchange for their funds.

- **Capital Expenditures**: Purchase of tangible property, such as real estate, equipment, and vehicles.

- **Working Capital**: Funds used for ongoing operating expenses of the business, including payroll, administrative and operating expenses, and marketing.

SOURCES AND USE OF FUNDS

Note: The total amount of financing being sought is $80,000 in equity financing. The company prefers that this entire amount be secured from only one investor. It is expected that these funds will be received and expended in early 2007. Thus the $80,000 is *not* reflected in the 2006 financial statements, but rather in the three-year projected income statement (page 120).

SOURCES OF FUNDS

Equity Investment	$80,000

USE OF FUNDS

Capital Expenditures

Leasehold Improvements	$ 5,000
Purchase of Equipment and Furniture	15,000
Total Capital Expenditures	**20,000**

Working Capital

Purchase of Inventory	5,000
Staff Expansion	25,000
Additional Marketing Activities	15,000
Other Business Expansion Activities	15,000
Total Working Capital	**60,000**

TOTAL USE OF FUNDS	**$80,000**

Answer the questions below to develop your "Sources and Use of Funds" statement.

SOURCES OF FUNDS

What is the total amount of financing you are seeking (investments and loans)?

How much are the principals investing?

How much will be in the form of equity investment from others?

How much will be in the form of debt financing, specifically bank loans?

What other forms of debt financing will you be seeking? (Include equipment, mortgage, and vehicle loans/leases.)

What other sources of funds are you seeking, if any?

USE OF FUNDS

How much are you going to spend on capital expenditures (such as real estate, equipment, or computers)? Specify use and cost.

How much are you going to spend on inventory?

How much are you going to spend on working capital to run your business (for example, marketing, staff, and operating expenses)?

5. Consider preparing additional supporting financial statements

Before you develop the four key financial statements, you may find it very helpful to create separate forecasts for a few major components of your income and expenses. If you're using your business plan for internal company planning, these planning tools are particularly useful.

If you're developing your business plan primarily to seek outside financing, you don't necessarily need to prepare these statements. However, doing so will help you find the numbers you need to put in your Income Statement and Cash-Flow Projection.

All of these supporting financial statements, and others, are included in the Electronic Financial Worksheets available for download purchase at The Planning Shop's website: *www.PlanningShop.com.*

Sales Projections

How many sales are you going to make? When? For how much? Forecasting your sales is obviously critical for understanding how much money you're going to have. Break down your projected sales by product line, on a month-by-month basis. Indicate how much you're going to pay in sales commissions, figure an amount for returns and discounts, and then calculate the cost of goods. This gives you revenue numbers to put in your Income Statement.

Staffing Budget

In many companies, the single biggest expense is the cost of employees. But it's often very frustrating (especially to investors) to see just one big number on the "Salaries" line of a financial statement. Instead, it's helpful to break down your personnel costs by category (management, production, administrative, and marketing, for example), indicating how many employees you'll have in each category and what they'll cost. This also gives you numbers to put in both your Income Statement and your Cash-Flow Projection.

Marketing Budget

If marketing is a major expense for your company, you may want to itemize how you plan on spending your marketing and advertising dollars. This budget can be helpful to you in your own internal planning even if you don't include it with the business plan you prepare for outside investors or lenders.

Your financial forms are a critical part of your business plan. Investors and lenders will turn to your financial statements quickly to measure your company's profitability and to see how you earn and spend your money. The four most important financial documents are your Income Statement, Cash-Flow Projection, Balance Sheet, and if you're seeking financing, your Sources and Use of Funds statement. If you're unfamiliar—or uncomfortable—with preparing financial forms, get assistance from an accountant or bookkeeper.

Putting Your Business Plan on Show

Once your written business plan is reviewed positively, you may be asked to meet with readers of your plan (such as potential funders) and give a presentation. It's likely that you'll want to prepare a PowerPoint or other presentation for that meeting.

This presentation should highlight the most compelling aspects of your business and answer questions such as:

☐ What is your business concept?

☐ What is the size and nature of your market?

☐ What's happening with your competition?

☐ Who's on your team?

☐ What are your financial projections?

☐ What kind of growth do you project?

For more guidance, see *Winning Presentation In A Day* available for purchase at bookstores and online at: **www.PlanningShop.com**.

Presentation
Pointers

Looks matter. While your plan will ultimately be judged on the quality of your business concept and your strategies for achieving goals, you also want to make sure it gives the best first impression possible. The way you prepare and present the document is itself an indicator of your professionalism. A polished plan sheds a favorable light on your company; a sloppy or incomplete presentation works against you.

Length of Your Plan

Don't burden your business plan readers with excess verbiage. Keep your business plan as short as is reasonable. Most businesses can keep their plans under twenty pages; those with particularly complex concepts or products should try to limit the plan to thirty-five pages maximum. Uncomplicated small businesses may not need twenty pages, but anything less than ten may seem a bit light. You can place additional information in appendices.

Format and Layout

- **Choose a clear font.** Most software programs offer many choices of fonts or typefaces. Choose one that's easy to read and professional in appearance. Generally, serif fonts (the kind with small lines or "feet" at the edges of each letter) make large amounts of text more readable, so choose this style for the body of your plan. Consider Garamond, Palatino, and Times New Roman.

Sans serif fonts (those without "feet") work well for headings and subheads, especially in a bold or condensed style. Try Arial, Franklin Gothic, or Verdana.

- **Use no more than two fonts in your plan**, and be restrained in your use of italics, boldface, and underlining. In terms of font size, 10- to 12-point type is best for body text; 12- to 14-point works well for headings and subheads.

Serif Fonts:	Sans Serif Fonts:
Garamond	Arial
Palatino	Franklin Gothic
Times New Roman	Verdana

Graphs and Charts

Graphs and charts are excellent tools for communicating important or impressive information. Place charts of half-page size or less within the text to capture your readers' attention. Produce some or all of your charts or graphs in color for more impact.

Since graphs and charts—especially those in color—attract attention, make certain you include only the most important or compelling information in the form of graphs or charts.

Here are some different types of charts you can use to help convey specific information.

Bar charts are useful when demonstrating trends or drawing comparisons:

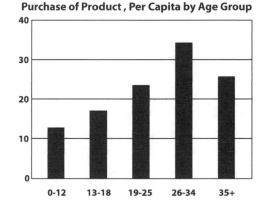

Purchase of Product , Per Capita by Age Group

Pie charts are ideal for showing the specific breakdowns of products sold, markets, etc.:

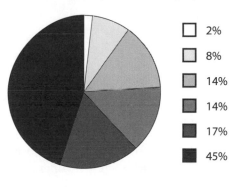

Store Sales by Product Category

- 2%
- 8%
- 14%
- 14%
- 17%
- 45%

Flow charts illustrate development patterns and organization of authority:

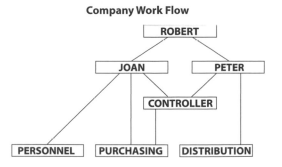

Company Work Flow

Binding

You can have your business plan bound for a few dollars at most copy centers. This will give your plan a more polished, professional appearance. If you decide to use presentation folders or report covers instead (available at office supply stores), choose a business-like color, such as black, grey, or dark blue. Label the front of your plan or use a clear cover with a title page. Readers should be able to see the name of your business without opening the plan.

Cover Sheet

Your cover sheet is the first thing readers will see when they open your plan. Make a good first impression with a clean, businesslike design. Your cover sheet should include:

- **Company name.**

- **Company logo**, if you have one.

- The words "**Business Plan**" in a prominent spot.

- The **name, address, phone number, and e-mail address** of the contact person

- **The date.** To be sure your plan doesn't look outdated, consider including only the year—or create a new cover sheet each time you send out the plan.

- **Copy number.** Number each copy of the plan you send out, and keep track of which reader (or institution) received it.

- **A disclaimer.** If you are circulating your plan to outside funding sources, you need to indicate that the business plan itself is not an offering of stock in the company. A disclaimer can protect you from legal problems and help protect the confidentiality of your plan.

A disclaimer might look like this:

This document is for information only and is not an offering for sale of securities of the Company. Information disclosed herein should be considered proprietary and confidential. The document is the property of _____ Company and may not be disclosed, distributed, or reproduced without the express written permission of _____ Company.

Consult an attorney for proper wording.

Appendix

An appendix allows you to include information at the end of your plan without bogging down the essential sections with too much detail. Some types of information you can include:

- **Positive coverage.** If your company has received any positive coverage in news articles or industry journals, supply copies or clippings.

- **Letters of Intent.** Any indication from customers or potential customers of their intent to do business with you—or such letters from potential strategic partners.

- **List of locations.** Useful if you have many different stores or branches.

- **Manufacturing descriptions.** Floor plans, flow charts, or other visual representations that describe your manufacturing process.

- **Marketing collateral.** Brochures, leaflets, and photos of packaging. You can also include market research reports and other industry data here.

- **Photos, Illustrations, Graphs, and Charts.** Any images showing new technology, unique packaging, impressive industry information (charts or graphs), or other highlights of your business that are better presented visually.

- **Technical information.** If you're developing a new technology, data sheets and other descriptions (which may be too lengthy or technical for the plan itself) may be helpful here.

Cover Letter

You must include a cover letter with any business plan you send or deliver to a potential funding source. The cover letter will probably be read before the recipient opens the business plan itself, so make certain it entices the reader to give careful consideration to your business.

If you are sending your business plan to someone who has requested it, your cover letter should indicate that fact: You can start with a simple sentence, such as

It was a pleasure meeting you last week. As you requested, I'm sending you a copy of my business plan, for my company,

_____.

Then continue to briefly describe your business.

If you don't know the recipient of your plan personally, but someone you know is connected to that recipient (an intermediary), the best way to start a cover letter is with this sentence:

_____ *(name of intermediary) suggested that I contact you regarding my business, _____ (name of business), a _____ (type of business).*

For example, the first sentence might read:

Phil Turner suggested that I contact you regarding my business, AAA, Inc., a food products and service company.

This immediately draws attention to the person connecting you to the funding source and gives you a measure of credibility.

Next, indicate why you (or the intermediary) feel that the recipient is an appropriate funding source. Continuing with the example above, the next sentence might read:

He knows of your experience in funding food product companies and believes you might find AAA, Inc. of interest.

If you don't have an intermediary and you haven't met the funder yourself, your first sentence should state the name and nature of your company and why you have chosen to send your plan to the recipient. It should read something like:

Knowing of your interest in funding food product companies, I am enclosing a copy of the business plan for AAA, Inc. We are an established food products and service company now seeking financing to enable us to expand operations.

Regardless of how—or how well—you know the recipient of your business plan, your cover letter should state:

- Why you've chosen the particular funder to receive your plan.

- The nature of your business.

- The developmental stage of your business.

- The amount of funds sought.

- Whether you are looking for an investment or a loan.

- The terms of the deal, if appropriate.

Keep your cover letter brief like the sample opposite. It should motivate the recipient to read your plan, not replace the plan itself.

Cover Letter Sample

Ms. Tamara Pinto
617 North Compton Boulevard
Vespucci, Indiana 98999

Dear Ms. Pinto:

My attorney, Mr. Kenneth Pollock, suggested I write to you regarding my business, ComputerEase. I am currently seeking an investor, and I believe that this company would coincide with your interest in technology-related service businesses.

ComputerEase is positioned to take advantage of the market opportunities presented in the corporate software training field. This is a relatively new field, and no companies yet dominate the market. ComputerEase, through a professional approach to marketing, experienced management, and an emphasis on outstanding customer support and service, can become the premier provider of software training in the Greater Vespucci area. From that base, the company will be able to expand to become a regional force.

We are seeking $80,000. We anticipate this will be the sole round of funding. The funds will be utilized to add one training center location, expand staff, and increase marketing activities.

I appreciate your consideration of the business plan for ComputerEase. I will telephone in approximately 10 days to see if you have any questions or to discuss how we may proceed.

Thank you.

Sincerely,

Scott E. Connors
President

Final Touches

The best business plans show up on their readers' desks with a clean design; clear, concise content; and an easy-to-navigate structure. Consider these additional guidelines for polishing and packaging your document.

- **Have it edited.** Ask someone with a good command of the English language to edit and proofread your business plan. After developing the plan yourself, you may find it difficult to catch typos and other grammatical problems on your own. You'll also want to see how others interpret your prose.

- **Include a table of contents.** If your plan is longer than ten pages, include a table of contents to help your readers quickly locate sections that interest them. Place it immediately after your cover sheet and before your Executive Summary.

Sending It Out

Before you drop your plan in the mail to any new financing source, give it another read-through, and if necessary, update it. Revise the plan to reflect recent developments (including new personnel), and bring financial information up to the close of the last month or quarter. Avoid printing too many copies at once so you're not tempted to send out an old plan just to get through the stack.

With investors and lenders in particular, your business plan is your calling card. Make sure its presentation puts the best face on your business and helps move your company closer to its goals.

Following Up

Your job is not done once you have sent out your business plan; you'll have to follow up with the recipients to make sure you actually receive an answer from your potential funding sources. Some banks or investors tell you exactly when you can expect to hear from them. Others are far less diligent in their communication. Don't be surprised if you're the one who has to take the initiative.

Don't become a pest, however. Keep your inquiries brief and professional, and don't contact potential funders too frequently. You can call for the first time about a week after sending your plan to make sure the plan has been received. During this first call, it's certainly appropriate to ask when you can expect to hear from the funding source or when you may call back. It's also acceptable to request an appropriate time to follow up again: "May I call back in two weeks to check on my plan's progress?"

Email and Voice Mail

Much of your interaction with potential funding sources will be through email and voice mail messages. Prepare what you want to say before you pick up the phone or hit the "Send" button.

Keep all your initial or uninvited emails and voice mails short. You have a better chance of having your message read or listened to if it is not too long. If you've worked on your "elevator pitch" (see page 151), you should be able to quickly explain the nature of your business.

If you have the name of an intermediary who suggested you contact the funding source, use that name right away, whether in a voice mail or email. In an email message, you might put the intermediary's name in the "Subject" line to make it more likely the recipient will open your message.

For a voice mail message, state the nature of your call and your business up front and then clearly and slowly tell the listener how they can reach you. Always indicate that you will also phone back. That gives you an opening to call again without seeming too pushy.

If you're trying to make initial contact with a potential funder, your voice mail message might be something like:

Phil Turner suggested I call you about my new food products and service company, AAA, Inc. Phil thought our approach to growth and our already-established customer base would interest you. I'd appreciate the chance to speak with you. I can be reached at 650-555-1000 or you can email me at arnie at aaa.com. I will also try you again in a couple of days. Thank you.

Your email message can be very similar to your voice mail. It should be short and direct, and you should provide a way for someone to contact you by phone. You can include the address of your Web site, if you have one up and running and you're willing to have the potential funder see it before they've talked to you. Refrain from using any attachments, especially in your first contact. Be careful not to be too vague in your "Subject" line. Don't use subjects such as "Great Business Opportunity" or "New Business Venture." You don't want your recipient to think your message is spam and delete it without ever opening it.

The "Elevator Pitch"

Before you meet with bankers, investors, or others, you need to work on developing your "elevator pitch." An elevator pitch is the term used for a very brief description of a company that an entrepreneur could give in the time it would take to ride up an elevator (and not an elevator in a skyscraper!). In your elevator pitch, you describe your company's product or service, market, and competitive advantages. An "elevator pitch" shows you understand your business. (If you're unclear about your strategic position, you'll still be mumbling as you pass the fifteenth floor.)

You'll use your elevator pitch over and over: in emails to prospective financing sources, to introduce yourself and your company at networking events, to describe your business to potential customers. So take a few moments to begin to develop your own elevator pitch.

My Company:

Named:

Does:

Serves Which Market:

Makes Money By:

Is Like What Other Companies:

Will Succeed Because It:

Aims to Achieve:

Nine Sure-Fire Ways
to Ruin Your Business Plan

1. Make basic mistakes

Leave out key information or get basic facts wrong, and you'll mess up your entire business plan. Do your homework so you're familiar with standard industry practices. Educate yourself about distribution channels, price mark-ups, regulations, and legal and accounting matters. One error can ruin all your projections and assumptions.

2. Underestimate the competition

The worst thing you can say in a business plan is "There is no competition." No matter how unique or terrific your product or service, if you don't have competition, it means there's no market for what you're selling. Be sure to consider potential future competition once you've proven the concept.

3. Overestimate sales

When you launch a product or service that's better, faster, or cheaper than the competition's, it's natural to assume customers will beat a path to your door. They won't. Be realistic, even conservative, about how difficult it will be to build a customer base and how long it will take.

4. Plan more than one business at a time

Even though your business may eventually have a number of revenue streams, concentrate on one part of it at a time. Show you can be successful in one area before branching out.

5. Go it alone

Nobody can build a successful business alone. Strategic alliances, particularly with strong existing businesses, can improve your chances of success. And if you want your business to grow, you'll need to attract and keep capable management and personnel. Show you can work well and creatively with others to leverage your resources.

6. Use "phantom" numbers

Don't use financial projections just because they sound good. Don't use "boilerplate" numbers: industry averages might not apply in your situation. Be able to substantiate where you got your numbers and why you made your financial assumptions. Always overestimate expenses and underestimate income.

7. Forget a "Sources and Use of Funds" statement

Financing sources want to see exactly how much money you'll need, how you intend to use it, what money you're contributing, and whether you are expecting to get funds from other sources. If you don't include this information in a clear, concise format, you'll confuse potential investors or lenders.

8. Omit an exit

While you may plan on running your business forever, others who invest in your company want to know how they'll get their money out. It's usually not enough for them to just get an annual return; they will want a way to make their original investment "liquid."

9. Lie

This is the best way to get a business plan rejected, increase the chances of your business failing, and ruin your reputation. While every business plan is developed with a certain degree of optimism, when the plan becomes fiction, you're in trouble.

The Experts Talk

Wouldn't it be wonderful if you could enter the minds of the people who will read your business plan—if you could learn what kinds of plans they read, what kinds they toss, and exactly what compels them to give a plan a thumbs up or a thumbs down?

Now you can. On the following pages, you'll find interviews with four people who read business plans for a living: two angel investors, a venture capitalist, and a bank loan professional.

They'll tell you in their own words:

- What kinds of information different financing professionals look for in a plan.

- What sections they turn to first.

- What they want to know about your team, your business, and your market.

- What aspects of a plan's presentation they like—and dislike.

- What could destroy your chances of getting financing or meeting your other objectives.

Some of the experts take you beyond the plan review, explaining what happens *after* a plan is accepted. They provide valuable information on the kind of involvement they seek in the companies they finance—as well as how the ongoing professional relationship between the entrepreneur and the financing individuals or institution really works.

Before you take your plan to your readers, learn from the experienced experts interviewed here. Their ideas will help you create a winning plan, determine exactly who should read it, and significantly boost its chances for success.

Tony Shipley, Angel Investor

Tony Shipley is Chairman of Queen City Angels, a Cincinnati-based group of investors focused on technology companies. He also serves as Chairman of CH Mack, a Cincinnati information technology company. He has extensive experience in entrepreneurial companies, having served as the CEO of a start-up that was later selected for the Inc. 500 list. He is a member of various business organizations and serves on numerous boards, including The Circuit and Ohio's IT Alliance. Tony Shipley has also won numerous awards for entrepreneurship and business achievement.

In general, what type of information do you, as an angel investor, look for in a business plan?

The first thing we want to know is: Does the product or service solve a specific customer problem, and what is that problem? Essentially, what is the *value proposition*? Then we'd also want to know who in the customer's organization *owns* that problem. In other words, who is the prospective target customer for the company?

Another thing we're interested in is management. When you're writing the check to fund an organization, at the end of the day, you're betting on the people. You need a strong belief that the management has the wherewithal to run the enterprise and execute the plan. Companies seeking early seed-type of investments, however, often have incomplete management teams. That's OK; we don't expect them to be a fully developed team at that point, but we expect the start-ups to recognize their limitations, to see the gaps in the team, and have a plan for filling them.

Also, when we invest, we've got to have a fairly clear vision of what the exit strategy looks like. We want to be able to get our money out in four to five years at the low end and in seven to eight years at the upper end.

What do you consider red flags or deal breakers in a plan?

A major problem is a proposed funding plan we feel is inadequate to allow the company to achieve certain milestones we believe are important to attract a follow-up round of investment.

Sometimes, entrepreneurs don't identify the person or group they're talking to in a customer's organization [their target customer]. That raises issues when it comes to evaluating their sales model.

A third problem occurs when the CEO or other executives are not "coachable." We learned a long time ago that no one knows everything, and we recognize the value in that. We like it when teams see their weaknesses and are willing to take input via our mentoring activities.

What type of business plan format do you prefer?

We ask that companies initially submit a five-page executive summary and an application. Entrepreneurs can find detailed guidelines on what should be included in the executive summary on our Web site: **http://www.c-cap.net/entrepreneurs.html**.

C-Cap is the administrative hub for our angel group. C-Cap staff members initially review the five-page summaries to make sure they have the essential format elements, then distribute them to the angel investors. This gives the angels a snapshot of the business model, and if that snapshot is compelling enough, we ask for the full business plan.

How long should the final business plan be?

We don't expect a dissertation. We find that the smarter people are, the more articulate they are and the more concisely they can write. In general, the main body of the plan usually runs about ten to twenty pages, but the appendices can make the plan quite thick.

What is the range of money you invest?

In our angel group, we're looking at the low end of $200,000 to $300,000 and the upper end of $1 million to $2 million.

What types of businesses do you fund?

We try to fund businesses in and around the Cincinnati area. As angel investors, we want to be close enough to jump in the car and drive to their site when they've got a crisis. We have found that most angel groups don't venture too far outside of their geographical area.

We tend to focus on technology companies and medical companies that have a tech orientation, like medical device companies.

How long does the whole process take, from the time the entrepreneur submits the plan to the time they get an answer?

With nominal due diligence [research], the whole process could last from three to six weeks. If we have to do in-depth due diligence, it could be several months.

What kind of role in the company do you expect when making an investment?

Our involvement varies, but we're not just about writing checks and walking away. Many of these companies are really in need of mentoring at this stage. At a minimum, we want to take board seats, but we also like to have people (angels) take advisory seats and offer consulting services. We feel it's important to provide hands-on involvement, to help entrepreneurs get over the hurdles that every new business must overcome. For us, stepping in and providing expertise is part of the fun. If we were just about writing checks, there are a thousand other ways for us to make money.

Patrick Sandercock, Banker

As a Relationship Manager with Harris Bank's Business Banking group, Patrick Sandercock works with companies and organizations with revenues of $10 million and less. He helps entrepreneurs, business owners, and managers better manage cash, finance capital investments, acquire businesses, and plan and execute succession.

Sandercock worked with two start-up businesses and completed research work published as a chapter in the text Entrepreneurship: The Road Ahead *(Rutledge Publishing). He has also co-facilitated a graduate-level course in technology commercialization.*

Patrick Sandercock received his B.S. degree (and commission) with a major in Government from the U.S. Coast Guard Academy in New London, Connecticut, and completed his M.B.A. with Distinction from DePaul University with a concentration in Entrepreneurship.

What type of information does a bank lender look for in a business plan?

In addition to much of the same information an equity investor seeks, a banker looks for cash flow that ensures repayment, as required by the loan structure. Banks also want the entrepreneur to list how he or she plans to use the borrowed funds. A "Sources and Use of Funds" section of the plan describes the various expenditures and the proportion of equity and debt to be applied. It establishes the overall size of the venture or project and how much funding will be provided by the bank versus the entrepreneur (or other equity source).

The bank may also be more interested in the entrepreneur's personal financial information than an equity investor. Banks use credit bureau scores as an indication of how the entrepreneur handles financial matters. If he or she is sloppy with repayment of home mortgage or personal credit card debt, then the bank may be concerned about how carefully the entrepreneur will attend to the business debt.

What do you consider the most important aspects of the plan?

First, an overall coherency. In other words, everything needs to "fit" and make sense. The various sections of the plan should build upon and support one another.

Second, the plan should clearly describe how the venture or project will exploit a market opportunity.

Finally, business plans can be great in theory, but require the execution of a management team with the right experience and expertise. Bankers look for a complete management team with backgrounds that connect past achievement with the venture's future.

In what order would you like the various sections of the plan to appear? What part do you read first?

The order is not terribly important as long as relevant information is included. I read the executive summary first. The most important sections supporting this executive summary include management's biographies (describing how past experience fits with future responsibility); operations, including sales tactics (describing how things will get done and revenue achieved); and financials (with particular attention placed on the assumptions that underlie the numbers).

What do you want to know about the competition?

I want to know how deeply the entrepreneur has researched the competition, and whether he or she has thought broadly enough to consider "substitute" products and services as indirect competitors. As has been described many times before, the Southwest Airlines business model considered not only other airlines as competitors but also bus lines along the same routes.

Secondly, the entrepreneur should describe his or her competitive advantage. In other words, why is someone going to buy from this new venture given other options?

What do you want to know about the market?

Many business plans describe huge markets and note that capturing a small percentage equates to large revenues, but this doesn't tell the banker why even one person will buy this product or service. The plan should describe the customer in detail and make clear how the venture's product or service meets the customer's need. The entrepreneur needs to show why the product or service is a compelling purchase to its target potential client, aside from the issue of how many potential clients are out there.

On a more "macro" front, the entrepreneur should describe the nature of the market (is it geographically specific? culturally-specific?) and make a connection between the market and the customer acquisition approach.

For example, if the entrepreneur has a snow removal product, the plan should discuss the target clients (likely in the north), and whether they are government, businesses, consumers, or a combination. Other sections of the plan will reinforce this market discussion by noting such things as when buyers' purchasing decisions are made (for example, what's the budget process for government customers?), seasonal cash-flow implications (such as how the company will meet obligations during summer months), and similar issues.

What do you consider red flags?

A plan that suggests there is no competition, or puts excessive focus on the potential financial return without enough depth on the operations and sales, raises a red flag.

What are some deal breakers? What will make you decide to reject a plan?

For banks, a venture is difficult to finance with traditional commercial bank debt if there is a long timeframe until profitability, insufficient equity invested by the entrepreneur or equity sponsor, or a lack of connection between the entrepreneur's track record and the proposed venture. Poor personal credit can be a deterrent as well.

What is the range of money you lend?

This depends in large part on the venture's scope, the equity available, and the ability to secure the debt with hard assets to the extent possible.

What kinds of business models most interest you?

As you might expect, banks typically prefer lower-risk business models. Ventures that generate cash flow quickly, involve hard assets, are franchise models with demonstrated success, are not environmental risks or ahead of the market's adoption of technology are often more attractive to banks than riskier opportunities.

How large are the companies you most often fund?

As a full service financial services provider, we provide financing for start-ups through major corporations.

Do you prefer that companies seeking money from you receive funding from other sources?

The company or entrepreneur should expect to bring some equity to the project either from existing operations (as when launching a new business line), from personal resources, or from an equity sponsor. As the lender, the preference for sole sourcing or participation will depend on the size and risk profile of the deal, as well as the lender's experience and comfort in the industry.

If possible, however, a bank will usually prefer to be the sole provider of the funding and maintain the entire banking relationship. This helps establish a clear priority of liens on assets (as security for the loan). In addition, seeing the entirety of a company's financial operations—deposits, cash management, investments, and debt—allows a bank to see opportunities for cost savings and efficiency improvements.

What do you notice first about a plan's physical presentation? What impresses you? What doesn't?

The plan's physical presentation gives some indication of the entrepreneur's respect for the old adage "You get only one chance to make a first impression." Typos, formatting errors, and inconsistencies indicate a lack of attention to detail.

The plan should be easy to navigate. A table of contents, heading structure, and references to other sections with related information, all show that the entrepreneur respects the reader's time and is interested in making his or her message as clear and coherent as possible.

Effective use of visuals is very powerful. Graphs, photos, charts, etc., all can help convey the plan's message clearly and persuasively.

That said, if the plan looks great but the content is weak, then this tells the banker there might have been too much attention placed on style rather than substance.

How long should the business plan be?

The executive summary (one to three pages usually) is a key part of the plan because— done right—this will bring all sections of the plan together in a way that is convincing, yet concise. Shorter, but well-constructed, is usually better than long-winded. Good bankers do not evaluate a venture based on the plan's physical weight!

How much and what kind of supporting data should be included (such as studies, surveys, graphs, and charts)?

This will depend on the venture. A more technical subject will likely require more support and education of the reader. The entrepreneur's most important goal is to ensure the supporting data has a clear connection to the venture's operations and projected success. A set of tables, graphs, or studies that describe a market beyond the venture's target market may actually confuse the issue and detract from the plan's message.

How much time do you spend reading a plan?

I spend thirty to forty-five minutes on average.

How long does the entire review process take (from the time businesses submit their plans, to the time they receive an answer)?

For a franchise opportunity, it might be less than a week from submitting a full loan request package to approval. Complex ventures might require several meetings,

discussion on aspects of the plan, discussions with equity sponsors and references, and "stress-testing" the financial model.

Is there anything you think entrepreneurs should know before submitting their plans?

The entrepreneur should detail the important underlying assumptions for the financial section. The plan should say:

- Why growth is expected at xx% and what will drive this

- At what point operational capacity is reached and new equipment (capital expenditure) or new hires (overhead) will be required

- What drives material costs; what trends are reflected in these costs; and how volatile these costs are

A discussion of "key challenges and contingencies" shows the entrepreneur has thought through what might go wrong and what he or she can do to respond. Rather than scaring a banker, the plan that presents the potential risks and how these can be overcome is a welcome sight.

Philip Schlein, Venture Capitalist

Philip Schlein is a partner with U.S. Venture Partners in Menlo Park, California. Phil joined USVP in 1985 after a successful twenty-eight-year career as an operating executive in the retailing industry. For eleven years prior to joining USVP, Phil was President and CEO of Macy's California. Under his leadership, sales grew from just under $200 million to almost $1.2 billion; profits grew from $17 million to $108 million. He also served on the Board of Directors of Apple Computer for eight years.

Since joining USVP, Schlein has originated a number of investments in the consumer/retail sector including PETsMart, Fresh Choice, and House of Blues. In recent years, he has served on the Boards of Directors of iVillage, HomeGrocer.com, and NBCi, among others. Phil Schlein currently serves on the Boards of Directors of Catalist, Specialtys, Auction Drop, and Oakville Grocery. He holds a B.S. in Economics from the University of Pennsylvania.

What type of information do you, as a venture capitalist, look for in a business plan?

The first characteristics we look for in a company is the quality of the management team. In all cases, it's important to have the references and to feel good about the people on the team. That's really significant. You could have a good, but not great idea, and a good management team will do what it takes to make it successful.

Then we look at the product. We ask: Is it something that's needed, or just nice to have? Needed means it's going to be really valuable; nice to have is not as valuable. If the product is a "need-to-have," and changes or enhances the way something is done, that indicates there will be a strong market for it.

Of course, the company has to have a business model that makes sense. How are you going to earn income? What are the revenue sources? We generally look at a five-year projection—we expect the first two or three years to make more sense, the last two or three to be a little more guesswork.

Market size and competition are the next important factors that must be considered.

Finally, we look at how much money is needed to take the business to a point where there could be an IPO or an acquisition. We look at the exit strategy and exit value. But that's only after we've looked at the other things first.

When you receive a plan, in what order do you read the various sections?

I might start by skipping back to see who the management team is. But I certainly want the executive summary up front to see what the company is all about and whether the business model makes sense. If they have patents or have applied for them, that also should be in the executive summary.

I want to see that there's a big enough market and how they differentiate themselves from their competition. Then I look at the financials to see if that validates the business model. They might have a summary financial in the executive summary, but the more detailed information is usually further back.

What do you want to know about the competition?

I want to know how the company is different from what's already out there, and what makes their product a "need-to-have." With technology, you have intellectual property that's protected. That's not the case with consumer businesses, which is why you really need an innovative idea and have to be able to execute it quickly.

What do you want to know about the market?

The size of the market is important. One could develop a great medical device for which there really isn't much need. When you look at the market, it may be so small, it's really not worth investing in.

What do you consider red flags?

Some things that would throw a business plan off include:

- A too-small market size

- Management that has no experience or involvement in a like business area

- A business or product that's not really needed

Sometimes the business model makes no sense, like when someone expects to go from zero to $100 million in two years. Some plans are just off-the-wall.

Do you get many plans that are "off-the-wall"?

The networking in the technology world is pretty tight knit. Usually the people sent to us are referrals, so we don't get as many off-the-wall plans there. It's different in the consumer world, though. I get plans that are off-the-wall, over-the-counter, onto-the-door, through-the-woods, and every other way. Sometimes, I don't even know the people they say referred them to me. I get a whole mixture.

What are some deal breakers? What will make you immediately decide to reject a plan?

It could be an unrealistic valuation* on the company. When we look at the exit value, it just doesn't make sense for us. Or the market might be too small for us. In that case, we might find smaller VC firms to help them. Sometimes, the plan just falls outside of what our core expertise and investment strategy is at any given time.

Valuation is the value of a company's stock based on its earnings and the market value of its assets.

What is the range of money you invest?

It really depends on the business, but $8-10 million is the minimum we would invest. We could have as much as $20 million in a business. We also invest in several rounds. For example, we might only have $1 million invested in a seed stage of financing.

What kinds of businesses most interest you?

We do life sciences, especially medical devices. We do semiconductors, telecommunications, software, enterprise technology. We don't do too much with companies selling direct to the consumer these days.

What size of companies do you finance, and at what stage do you come in?

For medical devices, we could come in reasonably early. With technology companies, it could be very early, maybe just at the point where they have the intellectual property. If it's a consumer business, we'd come in at a later stage, perhaps after they've opened two or three stores and some of the risk has been taken out of it. In many cases, we'd want the company to have at least one or two customers.

Do you prefer that a company's financing come mainly from you or from many different sources?

Most of the time, we have a VC partner. We might do something alone where we give some start-up money to a very early-stage company. Generally, we bring in partners, or they bring us in; it works both ways.

What do you notice first about a plan's physical presentation?

If it's too fancy, I get nervous, as I do when I walk into offices that are really fancy. I'd be wondering how they're spending their money. If a plan looked like a design firm put it together, I'd get nervous, unless it came from a very aesthetic business, which we usually don't invest in anyway.

What is a good length for a business plan?

The fewest number of pages needed to get the message across. If you think about it, you really don't need a lot. You can do an appendix with information that you don't necessarily have to include in the basic plan.

We get plans of all sizes. Sometimes, people go on and on, and are redundant, giving us fifty or sixty pages when it can be done in thirty. You begin to wonder if that person is focused, and focus is really important in the success of a company.

How much and what kind of supporting data should be included (such as studies, surveys, graphs, and charts)?

Again, it depends on the business. Pictures only help if they explain something or show how something works. Sometimes medical people have pictures to show how a device would work or how it would enter the body. In the consumer world, they could present pictures of the product line they're dealing with. Generally, though, it's what they say that matters.

How much time do you spend reading a plan?

It depends on the plan and what time of night it is. (I generally don't read anything in the office.) And it depends on how interesting it is, how pertinent it is; it's just like reading a book. In general, I just plow through all of them.

What type of involvement do you look for in the companies you finance?

In almost all of the cases, the businesses are fairly early stage, and we're on the board. But there are a few cases where a company is already more established and we aren't board members. We decide to invest anyway because we think the size is going to be good, and there are already other venture groups involved.

Enzo Torresi: Angel Investor

Enzo Torresi is the founder of EuroFund, a Silicon Valley–based firm that invests in seed and early-stage financing of software, communications, Internet, and wireless technology start-ups. He is also a partner in myQube, a high-tech venture fund based in Milan. Torresi has more than thirty years' experience in the computer industry and has founded six companies. He was listed among Fortune *magazine's Cool People of 2001.*

What kinds of companies interest angel investors (as opposed to venture capitalists and other investors)?

Angels tend to look at very early-stage companies where there's much higher risk. We provide the real seed financing. VCs nowadays go for the first or second round of financing, after the initial proof-of-concept stage. The first year of money is usually from the angels.

I finance companies that don't even have an office address yet. They have a concept, and they're shopping for money to get them off the ground. The only things that count at that stage are the idea, the founder, and the CEO.

What types of companies do you look for?

I mainly finance tech companies, those with intellectual property [such as patentable technology]. I don't do idea companies or dotcoms. The companies I most often fund are very small—the whole staff might consist of the CEO and CTO.

What is the range of money you invest?

Our investment is typically in the range of $50 to 100K. If you ask the other angels in Silicon Valley, they'd say $25K to 100K.

Do you prefer to be the sole initial investor in a company, or do you like to see financing from other sources?

I never do it myself. I like to have company—two or three other investors. Typically, when I decide to invest, I call some friends I've invested with before and tell them, "I saw something interesting. It's a good idea; send a check." They do the same with me.

What type of information most interests you in a business plan?

The founder's experience is very important. The only thing you can base your decision on is their track record, and how they make the presentation.

What kind of founder track record do you look for?

Everyone has different expectations, but I look at how many "bounces" they've had. If someone has had five employers in ten years, that's a warning signal to me. They usually say they're creative, or they've had bad bosses. I know someone can be trapped in a big corporate scenario with the wrong boss and decide to do something different after few years, but if it becomes a pattern, I tend to think it's a problem with them.

Lack of references is another problem. I've personally used the strategy of never burning bridges, which has helped me a lot. I'm skeptical of people who have lost contact with, alienated, or hate their previous bosses. I think it's a bad sign. If you can be a team player in a big company, that's a prerequisite to being a good manager. If you cannot be a team player, what's to say you can lead a team?

What do you consider the most important aspects of a business plan?

In general, the plan has to show the idea, the execution plan, and an analysis of the competition.

The most important part of the plan is the idea or description—the concept. It should not just show the knowledge or execution of the idea, but also what we call the *secret sauce*: What has this founder figured out that others have not?

You also want to know if there's a market, and if the idea can actually be executed. Somebody might say: "I have the idea of going to Saturn." Sure, there's a market, but it can't happen. There are a lot of naïve ideas that sound like this; they can't be done and are a waste of time. You'd be surprised how many entrepreneurs get defensive about that.

What do you want to know about the competition?

I want to know all *they* know about it. In many cases, I'll know more about a competitor than they do.

If someone tells me, "I have no competition," I get upset. I want to know why they think that. That's how I learn what the person understands about marketing, competition, and their customers. If I catch them underestimating, undermentioning, or not mentioning an obvious competitor, that's a big red flag. Some of them know they have competition; they just hate to admit it. Even worse are those who don't even know they have it.

In what order do you read the various sections of the business plan?

Well, everyone seems to follow some sort of template, but I first go to the management team section. The next thing I look at is the financial plan.

There's usually an opening statement. That's very important. Usually it's in the cover letter or somewhere at the beginning of the plan. If a company or a founder cannot articulate in a paragraph what they are doing, that's trouble. If they have to go into a convoluted five-page description of it, they're going to have problems explaining it to their salespeople and their sales partners. I think that's very common.

You mentioned three potential red flags: a questionable founder track record, a lack of a competitive analysis, and a convoluted concept description. What are some others?

Another one is a lack of a financial forecast. Often, entrepreneurs don't do one because they think it's too early. They say, "I don't know if I'm going to get the money, so I can't do a financial plan." I tell them, "You're also judged on how you make your assumptions."

An assumption could be: I'm going to raise a million dollars in VC financing; I'm going to hire a VP of marketing and a sales manager. Some entrepreneurs are afraid of getting nailed by the investors, of someone saying, "You're going to spend *this* much in a year?" But most angels and VCs know there have got to be some assumptions behind the plan. If you can't develop a financial plan until you get financing, that's a real problem, because everyone wants to know how you plan to spend the money.

What happens, then, if the assumptions, the idea, or the execution of the idea laid out in the plan change over time?

At the beginning, no company adheres exactly to the initial business plan. Many times, I've seen a complete reversal of the idea after giving someone money. It's not really a problem. I always say, if it's a smart team, they'll figure it out. They know the general direction in which they're going. It's much more of a problem if a company sticks to a particular course in spite of evidence that it's not going to work. Sometimes we call that *founderitis*, when founders are so consumed by an idea and won't change their minds.

I generally see the plan as a zigzag. You've just got to find the right *zig*. That's why, in the initial interview, I look for people who are flexible, to the point of admitting they might have the wrong *zig*.

Do you look for certain key words or buzzwords in a plan?

Generally, buzzwords are a turnoff, especially if it's clear the entrepreneur doesn't really understand the area. Buzzwords can actually raise a red flag; they open you up to more questioning. If you don't fully understand the concept, you can get nailed by the angel or VC reading a plan.

Never underestimate the knowledge of [the investors in] your audience. Chances are, once you go to present your plan, someone in the room is going to be an expert in the area you're talking about. If a CEO or CTO gives a presentation, and it's clear they don't understand the technology, that's instant death. I've never seen anyone recover from that.

What's an acceptable length for the business plan?

I prefer plans that are ten to fifteen pages; maybe twenty pages maximum. I don't know anyone who will read a thirty-page plan.

What kind of format do you prefer?

I like to see lots of graphics, like flow charts showing the architecture of a new technology. I don't like big blocks of text, but I don't like too many bullets either, unless they truly represent a concise way of looking at the concept.

Some business plans are really very badly written; they use long words, and long convoluted statements. A lot of people have a hard time putting their ideas down in ten pages, but to me, that's a test of how concise their thinking can be. I value conciseness.

What are your preferences regarding submission of the plan? Do you prefer mail? Fax? E-mail?

I get a lot of plans over e-mail. There's nothing I can do about it; people find out you're an angel or VC and start sending you their plans. I'm developing a theory that if I receive it by FedEx, it has a better chance. So I guess the hierarchy in terms of my preference would be: 1) FedEx; 2) regular mail, 3) fax; 4) e-mail. E-mail has made the unsolicited stuff much easier to broadcast for the creator, but it ends up in one big basket with all the Viagra ads and other spam. A good honest business plan could easily get lost in there.

How long do you spend looking at a business plan?

Well, on these unidentified flying objects as I call them [unsolicited e-mail plans], I spend very little time; I really just look at the cover letter. If it doesn't say in the body of the e-mail what they are doing, I don't even download the attachment. To me, it's very rude to send an attachment without saying what it is. If I do end up looking at the plan, I'll probably spend about five or ten minutes on it. I'll look at the concept, and see if I recognize any of the founders. If it's something that interests me, I'll usually give them a call right away.

So then how long does the entire process take, from the time you receive the plan to the time you make your decision?

With me, it can be as short as a couple of days. If the plan interests me, they'll come in for a presentation. It either happens at the presentation or it doesn't. In that forty-five minutes to an hour, you've got to make up your mind whether you trust your money to that person. That's really the bottom line. That's where I make my decision.

Business Terms
Glossary

Advisory Board: A non-official group of advisors; has no legal authority or obligation.

Angel: A private investor who invests personal funds in new enterprises.

Barriers to Entry: Conditions that make it difficult or impossible for new competitors to enter the market; examples include patents and extremely high start-up costs.

Board of Directors: The governing body of an incorporated company; this body has legal authority and responsibility for the business.

Capital: Funds/money to establish or run a business.

Cash Flow: The movement of money into and out of a company; actual income received and actual payments made out.

Collateral: Assets pledged in return for loans; examples include real estate and accounts receivable.

Corporation: A legal form of business that provides certain benefits for the company's owners, including protection from personal liability.

Cost of Goods: The direct costs to make or acquire products being sold; examples include the cost of raw materials or inventory.

DBA: "Doing business as." A company's trade name rather than the name under which it is legally incorporated; a company may be incorporated under the name XYZ Corporation but do business as "The Dew Drop Inn."

Debt Financing: Raising funds for a business by borrowing, often in the form of bank loans.

Distributor: Company or individual that arranges for the sale of products from manufacturer to retail outlets; the proverbial "middle man."

Equity: Shares of stock in company; ownership interest in a company.

Gross Profit: The amount of money earned after deducting the cost of goods but before deducting operating expenses.

LLC: Short for "Limited Liability Company," a specific legal form for a company providing limited liability and pass-through tax treatment for the company's owners.

Leasehold Improvements: Changes made to a rented store, office, or plant to make the location more appropriate for the conduct of the tenant's business.

Licensing Agreement: The granting of permission by one company to another to use its products, trademark, or name in a limited, particular manner.

Liquid Asset: An asset that can be turned into cash quickly and easily; examples include publicly traded stock and cash on deposit in banks.

Market Share: The percentage of the total available customer base captured by a specific company.

Milestone: A company's particular business achievement, such as shipping a new product or reaching a specific level of sales.

Net Profit: The amount of money earned after costs of goods and all operating and marketing expenses (often figured before taxes and depreciation).

Outsource: To have certain tasks done or products made by another company on a contract basis rather than having the work done by one's own company in-house.

Partnership: A relationship of two or more individuals to own or run a company without formal incorporation or the creation of an LLC.

Profit: The amount of money earned after expenses; it can be gross profit or net profit.

Profit Margin: The amount of money earned after expenses, usually expressed in percentage terms. *Gross profit margin* is the amount earned after deducting the cost of goods from total revenues; *net profit margin* is derived after deducting cost of goods plus operating expenses from total revenues.

Receipts: Funds coming into the company; the actual money paid to the company for its products or services; not necessarily the same as a company's total revenues.

Revenues: Total sales of a company before expenses. This is distinguished from profits or from receipts.

Sole Proprietorship: A non-incorporated company owned and managed by one person.

Strategic Partnerships: An agreement with another company to undertake business endeavors together or on each other's behalf.

Venture Capitalist: Individual or firm who invests money in new enterprises; typically this money is invested in the venture capital firm by others, particularly institutional investors.

Working Capital: The cash available to the company for the ongoing operations of the business.

Business
Resources

Funding Sources

Angel Capital Association— Directory

www.angelcapitalassociation.com/ directory.cfm

Directory of groups of angel investors throughout the United States and Canada.

Active Capital

www.activecapital.org

A non-profit organization designed to enable entrepreneurs to connect with angel investors via the Internet; originated by the U.S. Small Business Administration.

British Venture Capital Association

www.bvca.co.uk

The BVCA represents the vast majority of private venture capital firms in the United Kingdom.

European Venture Capital Association

www.evca.com

The EVCA represents over 950 venture capital firms in Europe.

Investors' Circle

www.investorscircle.net

A network of investors making private investments to socially responsible companies. They circulate proposals (for a fee) to their members.

National Association of Seed and Venture Funds

www.nasvf.org

An organization of private, public, and non-profit groups helping to create networks of investors in early-stage companies; also provides seminars for entrepreneurs.

National Association of Small Business Investment Companies

www.nasbic.org

Small Business Investment Companies (SBICs) invest in small businesses. A list of member companies is available from the site.

National Venture Capital Association

www.nvca.org

The NVCA represents the venture capital industry in the U.S. A list of member venture capital firms is available from the site.

Western Association of Venture Capitalists

www.wavc.net

The WAVC has more than 140 members, representing virtually all venture capital firms in the Western United States. A membership roster is available free by mail.

Entrepreneurs' Sources

The Planning Shop

555 Bryant Street, #180
Palo Alto, CA 94301
(650) 289-9120
fax: (650) 289-9125

www.PlanningShop.com

The Planning Shop, publisher of this book, is *the* central resource for business planning information and advice. In addition to information and tools for developing a business plan, The Planning Shop's Web site provides information on starting, growing, and running a business, including columns on entrepreneurship by Rhonda Abrams. You can purchase downloadable Excel spreadsheet templates of financial worksheets to assist you with the financial sections of any of our books at our Web site.

Association of Small Business Development Centers

www.asbdc-us.org

Over 1,000 SBDCs throughout the U.S. offer individual counseling, seminars, and technical help for entrepreneurs. Services are generally free. An outstanding, often overlooked, source of information for entrepreneurs.

Better Business Bureaus

www.bbb.org
www.bbbonline.org

A long-respected organization of businesses that agree to adhere to certain standards. BBBOnline offers a certification program for Internet sites to increase users' confidence in sites' reliability or privacy policies.

Entrepreneurial Edge

www.edwardlowe.org

Run by the Lowe Foundation, a non-profit organization dedicated to assisting entrepreneurs. Extensive website of resources and articles.

EntreWorld

www.entreworld.org

Developed and maintained by the private Kauffman Foundation, EntreWorld is a Web site providing information on a wide variety of topics related to entrepreneurship and starting and running a business.

FWE: Forum for Women Entrepreneurs

www.fwe.org

Founded in 1993, the Forum for Women Entrepreneurs (FWE) serves entrepreneurial women who are building or leading high-growth technology and life science companies. Started and headquartered in the San Francisco Bay area, the FWE also has chapters in Canada, Europe, and other U.S. locations.

Inc. Magazine and Web site

www.inc.com

A leading magazine for growing business. Inc.'s Web site offers a substantial archive of articles on business issues.

Microsoft Small Business Center

www.microsoft.com/smallbusiness

Microsoft's entry page for products and information for small businesses. Click on "Learning Center" to access articles and information on topics of interest to entrepreneurs.

NASE: National Association for the Self-Employed

www.nase.org

Membership organization providing a number of services to the self-employed and small businesses, including insurance and discounts.

NAWBO: National Association of Women Business Owners

www.nawbo.org

Membership group of women-owned businesses, with many local chapters around the country.

Quicken Small Business

www.quicken.com/small_business

Web site maintained by the company that makes Quicken financial software. Contains background information on many topics, particularly taxes and financial matters.

SCORE: Service Corps of Retired Executives

www.score.org

Provides retired business owners as counselors for assistance to individual entrepreneurs and conducts workshops on business skill topics.

SBA: Small Business Administration of the U.S. Government

www.sba.gov

U.S. government agency charged with the responsibility of aiding the cause of small businesses. Primary responsibility is administering guaranteed loan program. The SBA itself does not give loans; SBA loans are made through banks.

Software Developers' Forum

www.sdforum.com

Long-standing, well-regarded group of Silicon Valley entrepreneurs, working primarily, though not exclusively, in high tech. Sponsors or co-sponsors many seminars and programs on general entrepreneurship and start-up issues. Conducts one-on-one meetings with venture capitalists.

Index

Acknowledgments

Rhonda Abrams and The Planning Shop would like to thank:

Julie Vallone, who brought her constant professionalism, expert writing skills, easy-going personality, and good humor to this project. Julie has been an outstanding addition to The Planning Shop team, and we look forward to a long working relationship with her.

Mireille Majoor, our Editorial Project Manager. Mireille has overseen the entire development process, managed too-tight schedules, and risen to the challenges of creating a new editorial process. We have benefited greatly from Mireille's knowledge of the publishing process, good humor, unending patience, and her occasional pun.

Arthur Wait, who is responsible for the look and feel of everything carrying The Planning Shop name. We are always amazed (though no longer surprised) at the range of his talent. As VP of Everything (not his real title, but it should be), Arthur has his hand in shaping the entire direction of The Planning Shop, as well as being its tech wizard.

Diana Van Winkle, who brought her graphic expertise to improving and refining the design of this book. Her rapid responses and professionalism made working with her a pleasure, and she shares in the credit for making this book as elegant and user-friendly as it is.

Deborah Kaye, the "glue" that holds The Planning Shop together. Not only does Deborah manage all relations with the academic market, but she oversees operational issues and handles all the challenges that arise.

Brian Luce, who makes sure that the books get shipped, the phones get answered, the bills get sent, and otherwise handles the day-to-day administrative details of The Planning Shop's busy office.

The experts who provided such valuable, real-life insight into the business plan evaluation process: Tony Shipley, Patrick Sandercock, Phil Schlein, and Enzo Torresi. Special thanks to my good friend Phil, who has provided guidance and assistance for many years as well as being my standing date for Opening Day every year for the San Francisco Giants.

Kathryn Dean, who brought her eagle eye and expert judgment to the editing and proofing process, and who created the index in record time.

Finally, thanks for the company and support of the three amazing dogs at The Planning Shop: Cosmo, Ozzy, and Nana. Woof!

Julie Vallone would like to thank:

My daughter, Siena, for spilling juice on my keyboard when it was clearly time for a writer's break; our cats, Zoe, Squinky, Lola, and Sappho, for keeping my feet and pages warm; and my husband, Rick, for patiently putting up with the stacks of disheveled paper and books, scattered energy bar wrappers, and thirty-four used coffee cups littering our dining table as deadline approached.

My gratitude also to designer and Web wizard Alan Luckow, who knows how to connect, and to the kind folks at Mr. Toots, The Ugly Mug, and Union coffee houses in Santa Cruz County, my satellite offices.

Notes

Notes

There's more where this book came from!

Ask your bookseller about these other **In A Day** titles from The Planning Shop, or buy direct at www.PlanningShop.com

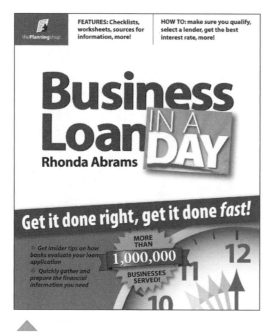

Securing a loan can be one of the biggest financial steps you take for your business. This unique book takes you through the often-confusing process of determining how much you need to borrow, selecting an appropriate bank, negotiating a favorable interest rate, and much, much more.

When you've got to wow an audience—whether it's making a persuasive sales presentation to a key customer, an internal report to senior management, or a motivational keynote to a packed auditorium—this book will help you get prepped, pumped, and ready to go—fast.

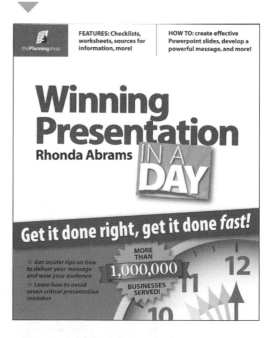

You've got a business plan: Now what?

You've finished *Business Plan In A Day* and have a winning business plan, ready for implementation. Now you're ready to get your business started!

Six-Week Start-Up is carefully designed to show you, step-by-step, how to get your business up and running—*quickly* and *successfully*.

From licenses to bookkeeping to marketing to hiring employees to setting up shop, this book guides you through every critical step, ensuring that you understand how to take care of even the smallest details. Nothing is left to chance—you'll be given all the information you need, as you need it.

The book is divided into six main chapters—one for each week—allowing you to pace yourself and take care of each task in its proper sequence. The book's unique

format significantly streamlines the start-up process, allowing you to start making money faster.

Book features:

• **Week-by-week checklists:** See exactly what you need to do on a weekly basis, along with detailed information on how to complete each item.

• **"Red Tape Alerts":** Stay out of trouble in areas related to taxes, laws, employment regulations, and more.

• **"Questions to Ask":** Before you meet with accountants, lawyers, investors, or other professionals, review these lists of important questions to ask.

It's all here! Get your business up and running fast! Order your copy of *Six-Week Start-Up* today.

Available from your bookseller or at www.PlanningShop.com

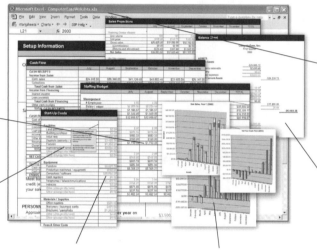